"Michelle Siteman's w... raising a musical child... parent dealing with the... young musician."
--*Jeffrey Kahane, Music Director of the Colorado Symphony Orchestra and the Los Angeles Chamber Orchestra.*

"In a clear and straightforward manner, Ms. Siteman offers insight and practical suggestions for advancing the development of musically talented children. This is a most useful and valuable book for anyone who is raising such a child or, for that matter, for anyone who is simply curious about the joys and frustrations of dealing with musically gifted youngsters."
--*Gary Graffman, President Emertius of the Curtis Institute of Music*

"As a 'Wunderkind,' I too had experienced all the difficulties a young musician faces in school—when there is simply not enough time to practice for hours and also fulfill a pupil's obligations and requirements: a real struggle. This book hits the nail right on the head! It could really help and guide parents of young musicians to cope with the problems arising in these situations. In addition, the book is written beautifully—with rich, expressive language that makes it a genuine pleasure to read."
--*Yoav Talmi, Israeli Conductor/Composer*

"Michelle Siteman's new book is a fascinating look at the varied ways we grow up to become musicians and the joys and obstacles encountered along the way."
--*Steven Copes, Concertmaster of the Saint Paul Chamber Orchestra*

"[This book] contains all the details parents need to navigate successfully in the waters of classical music training, and it is written in a personable style that makes it non-threatening. I find it impressive and helpful in every way…Music teachers should read this to better understand the student/teacher psychological dynamic… Truly excellent!"
--Anne Diener Zentner, Principal Flutist, Los Angeles Philharmonic

"Michelle Siteman is insightful, experienced, very smart and funny. It's a breath of fresh air to read a book on this complex, emotional subject by someone who's been there and done it. Successfully. If my wife and I had been non-musicians, and if Ms. Siteman's book had been around when our daughter was little, it would have been the most important book in our library."
--Ian Freebairn-Smith, Grammy Award-winning composer, long-time classical music radio host

THE PLEASURES AND PERILS OF RAISING YOUNG MUSICIANS

A Guide for Parents

by

Michelle Siteman

Bloomington, IN   authorHOUSE®   Milton Keynes, UK

AuthorHouse™
1663 Liberty Drive, Suite 200
Bloomington, IN 47403
www.authorhouse.com
Phone: 1-800-839-8640

AuthorHouse™ UK Ltd.
500 Avebury Boulevard
Central Milton Keynes, MK9 2BE
www.authorhouse.co.uk
Phone: 08001974150

© 2007 Michelle Siteman. All rights reserved.

No part of this book may be reproduced, stored in a retrieval system, or transmitted by any means without the written permission of the author.

First published by AuthorHouse 3/23/2007

ISBN: 978-1-4259-6886-1 (sc)

Library of Congress Control Number: 2006909361

Printed in the United States of America
Bloomington, Indiana

This book is printed on acid-free paper.

Table Of Contents

Acknowledgements	vii
Introduction	ix
Chapter One: Raising A Young Musician: My Personal Story	1
Chapter Two: First Signs Of Talent	13
Chapter Three: You Want To Play The What?	29
Chapter Four: Helping Your Child Select The "Right" Instrument	51
Chapter Five: Obtaining An Instrument	73
Chapter Six: Life At School	83
Chapter Seven: Practice Makes Perfect	99
Chapter Eight: Private Teachers	125
Chapter Nine: Cost And Benefit Analysis For Parents	145
Chapter Ten: Going Pro	163
Chapter Eleven: Academic And Intellectual Benefits Of Music Study	177
Chapter Twelve: The Social And Personal Benefits Of Studying Music	189
Appendix: Overview of the Orchestra	207
Endnotes	221
Index	227

Acknowledgements

Many wonderful people have helped me in the writing of this book. Marianne Smith, whose children studied music with mine, encouraged and sympathized with me throughout the sometimes tempestuous years of our children's musical adventures. She was both my muse and my parental sanity barometer. Without her support, understanding, and insight, I would never have finalized this "writing project."

Scores of parents raising musical children from across the country were excited about the prospect of collecting our experiences for the benefit of others. They shared with me their recollections, anxieties, and frustrations, their confusions, joys, and breakthroughs—the heart of this book. I thank them and honor them.

Kathy Jackson worked to free me from demeaning pedantry, Judith Aftergut untangled awkward prose, Nurit Caspi provided a teacher's perspective, and Zelda Freeberger caught wayward punctuation with a keen eye.

My gratitude to John Bach for his design ideas and a special thanks to my brother, Frank Siteman, whose photographs illustrate the text and whose encouragement kept me going.

A big thank you to my husband and three children who inspired me to undertake this project, who lived these experiences with me, and who have finally stopped asking, "When will you finish that book?"

Introduction

As the mother of a child who became a classical musician, I had issues that were not discussed at PTA meetings. Private music teachers were generous with their time and advice, but I wasn't a musician and I needed more help than they could provide. There seemed to be right ways of doing things, but I didn't know what they were. I was often adrift, wondering what was expected. Was I adequately meeting eight-year-old Jonathan's needs or was I over-indulging his expensive tastes? Was my son "normal"? Was I?

I began interviewing other parents who had raised musicians and found they had difficulties similar to mine. Parents from all over the country eagerly shared their stories with me. They described their confusions, their frustrations, their anxieties, and yes, their joys. These families often felt isolated, so they relished the opportunity to talk to a kindred spirit about their children.

I collected their stories as a testament to our shared experiences. This is the book I wish had been available to me when Jonathan was young. In it, you will read my stories about Jonathan and stories other parents told about their children. You will read about the nasty battles we fought, the surprising discoveries we made, and the quirky solutions we hit upon. This book is also intended for parents who would like to give their children a musical education but aren't sure how to begin. Several chapters address the many benefits that music education bestows on parents as well as their children.

If, when I was raising Jonathan and tearing my hair out, I had had a mentor to guide or reassure me, I might have survived the experience with healthier hair. I needed a "support group" but no such animal existed. I needed, not so much information (although that was very important) and not so much advice (although I was grateful for whatever I could get), but simply the comfort of knowing others had traveled this path before, and assurance that my son was not terribly abnormal.

I hope this book will serve as a road map for those who are now hurtling through life with a musical child and also for those who wish to enter that fascinating and rewarding territory. The information in it should reassure you. You will learn what the lay of the land is like—where the bumps in the road are likely to jut out and rattle you, where you need to keep your foot steady on the gas pedal, and where you better just shut your eyes and let the thing drive itself. If you can relax, you will certainly enjoy the trip.

CHAPTER ONE

RAISING A YOUNG MUSICIAN: MY PERSONAL STORY

My experience raising Jonathan is the reason for this book. It is only in retrospect, however, that I see it as a story. Living it was something else. Sometimes amusing, sometimes sweet, but mostly baffling, Jonathan was difficult for me. I had a handle on my two older children and could navigate the calmer waters of their childhoods, but raising Jonathan challenged my competency as a mother.

There were signs from the beginning that this child would not be easy. The night before I gave birth to Jonathan, I waddled into the Dorothy Chandler Pavilion in Los Angeles for a performance of Verdi's Requiem. Throughout the concert, whenever the big drums sounded, they were accompanied by my baby's kicks, making it hard for me to concentrate on the music. This memory remained vivid for years, but only later did I reinterpret it as the earliest sign of Jonathan's musicality.

As a baby, Jonathan was mesmerized by the music coming from speakers in our living room. When the music started, he would stand close to the speakers and sway to the different rhythms. When the music stopped, he would stop swaying, look up plaintively, and ask for more "mumik." He exhibited the same behavior when someone began to sing. He would turn abruptly from whatever toy he was playing with, walk purposefully over to the singer, stare, and ask for more.

He demonstrated a real affinity for music when he was only nine months old. There was that evening in the dining room when Jonathan, seeing that we were preparing for our customary Friday night dinner ritual, began singing the blessing over the wine. He couldn't talk at the time, but he could sing that melody and we found it funny, amazing, and more than a little wonderful.

When he was a toddler, I took him to "Mommy and Me" classes where the teacher played the zither, sang songs, and tried to use both hands to dramatize. The itzy bitzy spider was always climbing up that garden wall. Later I took him to a Yamaha Music Class next door to a McDonald's on Santa Monica Boulevard where his teacher, Miss Annie, took attendance by playing "Twinkle, Twinkle Little Star" on the piano and singing, "Johnny, Johnny, are you there?" He responded: "Yes, Miss Annie, I am here." Waiting until the next week when he could be "there" again was the problem. Several times a week I would hear, "Can we go to Miss Annie today, Mommy? No? When can we go to Miss Annie, Mommy?"

I enjoyed taking my two older children to Saturday morning children's concerts given by the Los Angeles Philharmonic and always brought Jonathan along. He was only two when he first started going. While my older children certainly enjoyed the concerts, they also enjoyed squirming and staring at all the dressed-up people in the audience and at the ornate ceiling. Jonathan would sit transfixed until the end of the piece when he would remember to breathe, turn to me, and ask, "Will they play another song, Mommy?"

Chapter One: Raising A Young Musician: My Personal Story

So I knew that he enjoyed music.

At the beginning of third grade, his school sponsored a "Meet the Instruments" program which had a profound effect on his life. Many different instruments were played and displayed and, at the end of the presentation, the children were encouraged to come up on stage and take a closer look at them. Jonathan announced that he wanted to play the one with all the buttons. He approached the young man who had introduced all the wind instruments and told him so. The young teacher obliged by opening several cases and asking Jonathan which one he meant. He showed my son the clarinet and the oboe. "No," Jonathan said, "shinier." He opened the trumpet case. No, Jonathan said, longer. He opened the flute case and Jonathan said, "Like those, but longer."

Now the flute, when not in use, is broken down into three smaller tubes and stored in a hard case. These were the three parts Jonathan was looking at. "OK," said the nice man. "Like this?" and he screwed the parts back together making one long flute. "Yes, yes, that's right!" said Jonathan. He beamed with pleasure and for the next 14 years he played the flute.

I never knew what made Jonathan, at the age of eight, certain that he was a flutist, that he had to play this and only this instrument. (Although later he learned to play several other instruments.) Once, when a family friend asked him if he wouldn't prefer the violin, Jonathan explained: "Stringed instruments are boring to play, since they only have four strings. But the winds! You play them using your *life* breath." Later, when he was 12, he wondered aloud what would have happened to him if he had made a "mistake" and picked another instrument! Another time he asked, "What if I am really a clarinetist who only *thinks* he is a flutist?" Shades of Kafka, you say, but Jonathan was dead serious. You will read later about other children who displayed a similar clairvoyance about what instrument they were meant to play.

3

Jonathan took flute lessons from Susan, a wonderfully warm teacher who lived not far from us. The night she first brought him his own beginner's instrument, he took it to bed with him. His grandmother thought that was a bit much and discouraged it, but we just thought it was funny. Now I realize that it was love. I don't remember how many nights he slept with his flute, but he adored it as well as his teacher.

It was a very happy time for him. During these years he also wanted to take piano lessons, which I agreed to for a time but later discontinued because the costs were mounting.

For one thing, there was the small matter of maintenance. Flutes have pads that wear out and need repair and replacing. Getting them fixed requires finding the right repair person and paying for his highly specialized services. At one time the only repair person who Jonathan would trust to work on his flute was located in San Francisco. We had to mail the instrument to him and pray for its safe return.

Then there was the larger matter of more sophisticated and therefore more expensive instruments. The beginner's flute worked well enough until Jonathan got to a level of performance that demanded a better instrument. Good flutes can cost several thousand dollars. (The cost of flutes, however, is modest compared to that of string instruments.)

There was another major matter: *keeping* the instrument. The flute is not so large that it cannot be misplaced, hidden, or forgotten somewhere. Since elementary-school children are known for losing their lunches and their sweaters on a regular basis, it should come as no surprise that they occasionally lose their instruments.

Once at work I got a frantic call from my son: he had left his flute on the bus on the way to school! What to do? I panicked—because of the cost of the instrument and the difficulty of finding a suitable replacement. I spent the rest of the day calling pawn shops, hoping it would show up. But we were lucky. We got a call later that day from a high-school student asking if we had lost a flute. He had found one on the bus and wanted to return it to us! Ricardo was a clarinetist so he knew that the owner of this flute would be pacing nervously. When we met him to pick up the flute, he absolutely refused to accept any reward money for recovering it.

Another problem in those years concerned practicing. That dirty little word. Jonathan hated to practice. I hated reminding him to practice. One afternoon, our negotiations about when he would start his practicing exploded into a full-blown battle, complete with screaming, feet-stomping for emphasis, and ugly threats. I threatened him with the loss of music lessons if he didn't practice. He called my bluff and said, "Fine!" I told him to pick up the phone and tell his teacher that he wasn't continuing, but he couldn't do it. He loved the music part of it—just not the hard work. So ended the melee, and after it we held to a partial truce, but the matter was never really settled until years later.

Throughout his elementary school years, Jonathan just got by. He did as little homework as he could get away with, and practiced his flute only when an upcoming recital forced him to. His primary goal those years was simply to fit in with the crowd. Since his crowd did hockey and skateboarding, Jonathan did, too. He got some good exercise, but his effort to "fit in" never really worked. It hurt to watch my child trying to figure out how to be "popular" and dealing with daily rejection. I simply could not understand how it was possible that other kids didn't "like" him.

Those were difficult years, but they ended decisively the summer of sixth grade, when he found a small music camp in the San Bernardino Mountains, situated between Lake Arrowhead and Big Bear resorts and called, fittingly, Arrowbear Music Camp. This one-week session changed his life.

At the end of the week, when parents came to hear their children perform in the camp orchestra, Jonathan met me and took me for a private, pre-concert walk in a rocky wooded area. We walked holding hands and he said, "At this place I like everyone, and everyone here likes me! Really, Mom!" He had found a place where he "belonged." When we walked back to the center of camp where the campers were preparing for their concert, I heard a cute blond girl excitedly call out his name.

That was the beginning of his love affair with this unassuming camp (and the cute blond). For many summers afterwards, he begged to go there, for play or for work. The last summer there he not only played chamber music, but also moved cots, built stairs, and poured concrete. He would have done anything that allowed him to stay there, playing music in those woods.

When I came up at the end of that first summer for the chamber music concert, I was introduced to Rosemarie, the woman in charge of the program. She stopped me short with the question: "Are you a musician? No? Well, your son is and you need to get him what he needs." What were those needs? She elaborated. Jonathan needed an orchestra to develop his "musicality." I didn't know what that word meant. "He is a very talented boy," she asserted, "and he *must* have the appropriate education."

I looked up the word, took her earnest advice, and searched for an orchestra in our neighborhood. There was no serious orchestra for 12-year olds within a half-hour's drive from our house. That is how a new chapter in our life opened. At Rosemarie's urging, Jonathan auditioned for, and was accepted to the Pasadena Youth Symphony Orchestra, a fine middle-school orchestra supported generously by the community. Unfortunately, it was not *our* community, and involved a drive across Southern California. It rehearsed once a week and no student was allowed to miss a rehearsal unless they were ill. Doctor's note required.

Every Tuesday afternoon, I would pick up Jonathan from school and drive down three freeways to Pasadena where we grabbed a quick, early dinner before he had to be in his assigned seat with his flute

Chapter One: Raising A Young Musician: My Personal Story

ready for the "downbeat" at 5:00. I was then free to roam the streets until the end of rehearsal at 8:30, when we piled back into the car for the long trip back home. At the end of the day, both of us were exhausted, but Jonathan loved it. I loved that Jonathan loved it and soon found ways to pass the time: grocery or clothes shopping, dinner with another mother, occasionally a film showing in the right time frame.

Though this weekly routine was tiring, what bothered me more was the way so many friends and family criticized my driving Jonathan so far just to play in an orchestra. "Why does it have to be that orchestra and not another, less illustrious one close to home?" "Why do you spoil him?" "Aren't you being over-indulgent?" "What about you and your needs?" "Why do you make yourself his slave?" These questions felt like attacks and they persisted for years. I learned to defend myself, parrying accusatory questions with defensive answers: "I enjoy the time with my son." "It makes him so happy I can't say no." "There is no orchestra like this at home" "I enjoy discovering a new part of California."

Jonathan (and I) continued with this orchestra for three years.

One of the requirements regional orchestras make of their students is that they participate concurrently in their local school orchestras. This was a different challenge. The high school Jonathan attended had a small beginners' orchestra which he considered a waste of time. I considered his attitude condescending and obnoxious. In fact, this became a theme during his high school years and caused a great deal of turmoil in our lives: Jonathan considered many requirements made by high school to be a waste of time and he simply would not do them. Homework, for instance. Class attendance, for another. There were many fights at home and it only got worse with the years, coming to a head several years later when he started preparing for college auditions.

The school orchestra director was a nice man and the orchestra students were great, but playing the flute with beginners who were just learning the notes was torture for him. The only reason Jonathan remained in his high school orchestra was that it was a requirement of the regional Pasadena Orchestra. First he tried negotiating his way out: "What if he was allowed to do his homework during rehearsals?" "What if he was allowed to use the practice room for his own practicing during rehearsals?" "No, no, and no." Finally he hit on something that would work. He wouldn't play the *flute*! Nothing in the rules said he had to play his *own* instrument. Instead, he would play the string bass! He was a rank beginner on the bass, so playing it in his high-school orchestra was an appropriate challenge for him. And, as a bonus, he was learning to read the bass clef. Problem solved.

If only other school issues could have been solved so neatly. Next came a showdown of sorts with the athletic department. Jonathan loved water sports and was on his high-school's water polo team. At least for a short while. The issue here was that team games conflicted with flute lesson times. By ninth grade, Jonathan was taking flute lessons with the principal flutist of the Los Angeles Philharmonic and she taught only on Saturdays when the water polo team often had games. Jonathan proposed that he be allowed to remain on the team, if only for the practices. He was willing to miss competing in the matches, but he felt he could not miss a flute lesson. His coach felt he could not miss a water polo match, could not remain on the team if he couldn't participate in the matches, and issued an ultimatum to that effect. Jonathan responded by dropping out of the water polo team and, for good measure, dropping out of school.

I exploded. I was not what was then called a "permissive" parent, so the general lines of the battle can be easily surmised. I believed in education. I believed in rules. I believed in following through. I believed in *normalcy*. I believed in "parenting," in setting limits and offering alternatives. Above all, it seemed, I believed in a high-school diploma.

Jonathan believed primarily in himself. He calmly informed those of us who took issue with his decision that he would be willing to go

Chapter One: Raising A Young Musician: My Personal Story

to a school if it offered him what he needed: time for his music. He researched and found a magnet school that specialized in music. Now, instead of attending a well-endowed suburban school, he would be attending a crowded inner-city-like school where two math students shared the same textbook. This was not what I had dreamed of. To further complicate matters, he would need to use a "fake" address if he wanted the privilege of attending this school. Doing this was not easy for a play-by-the-rules mother. But Jonathan, with the help of his grandmother who lived in the "right" area, made the necessary arrangements. He applied and got in. He made the switch in time for the second half of his sophomore year and I breathed a cautious sigh of relief. I was not thrilled about the switch, but at least my son would get a high-school diploma. Or so I thought.

There was a short period of relative calm during which the biggest issue was Jonathan's refusal to do any homework that he felt he didn't need to do. He patiently explained, "If I have time after I finish practicing, I'll do the homework." His arrogance and stubbornness drove me up the proverbial wall.

From this account of how hard he worked to get enough practice time, one might have the notion that Jonathan had learned to love practicing. Or at least that practicing had become easy for him. But this was not the case. Once, when he was only ten, he implored, "Mom, when I say I don't want to practice, please make me do it anyway." What had happened is that, mid-way through high school, he had decided that he wanted to become "the principal flutist of a major American orchestra." He realized that he would be competing for one of the very few spots at a top conservatory, and to get there meant he had to practice seriously and systematically. He and his teacher settled on five hours a day. One hour before school. One hour during school. Two hours after school. One hour before bed. His teacher thought he might have a chance at becoming a professional flutist and encouraged him. I was willing to go along with it but thought he was exaggerating what was necessary.

This is why homework became an issue. After practicing, he really didn't have a lot of extra time. Nor did he have a lot of fun. Having time for fun was an issue of mine. When we took a family vacation to Eastern Europe (the summer before he planned to audition for college), Jonathan agreed to go only if we could promise him at least three hours of practice time each morning. While the rest of the family went out sight-seeing, Jonathan would closet himself in the hotel room and practice until noon when he agreed to join us to see something of Prague and Vienna. I thought he was taking things a bit too far. His brother and sister thought he was nuts.

His tenure at the music magnet school, while never all that promising, lasted only a year and one semester. At the end of his junior year, Jonathan's counselor phoned to inform us that, in order to graduate, Jonathan needed to take two required courses, one in health and another in "life skills." I saw no problem with that, I told her. "Oh," she said, "but he does and he is refusing to enroll in them." At the conference with the principal the next morning, it became clear that the school would not allow Jonathan to continue into his senior year without these courses on his schedule card. Jonathan proposed a compromise. He would take the final exam to see if he could "place out" of these courses. No, said the principal, that couldn't be done; there was an attendance policy. So Jonathan thanked him and said he was sorry he would have to leave. I said nothing—my teeth were clenched.

Jonathan felt he would be perfectly satisfied staying home that year, reading on his own, and practicing. I felt less than satisfied with that proposition because I really wanted my son to have a high school diploma. It was then that he informed me that he would not need one for anything important to him.

"All I really need, in order to get into a top conservatory," he told me calmly, "is one very good audition. They don't care about grades or about teacher recommendations and they won't be asking to see my high-school diploma."

Chapter One: Raising A Young Musician: My Personal Story

'But what if you don't get in?" I asked.

"Then I'll try again the following year."

"But what if you just don't get in?" I pleaded. "What about a Plan B that includes a college education?"

"Mom, I don't want a Plan B. People who have a Plan B usually wind up following it."

He was determined to be a professional flutist and no amount of arguing had an effect. Nevertheless, I looked for yet another school for his senior year and found we were running out of schools. The one I found was an "alternative" school serving a student population of pregnant teen-agers and my son. There he could stop by once a week to drop off his old assignments, pick up his new assignments, and, best of all, he would have to be there only an hour a week! He went willingly.

So September started with Jonathan going to high school one hour a week, practicing the flute several hours a day, and with me at work worrying about him all day. This sorry state continued for several weeks until one day in October, when Jonathan got a call from an international music academy. They asked if he would like to join their orchestra. It seems they needed a principal flutist.

I had heard about this academy but had never considered sending my son there, first because of the steep tuition and second, because it was a boarding school and would mean his leaving home. But now they were offering him a full-tuition scholarship, a high-level of music making, and academic classes as well. They even offered high-school diplomas! I was sold. He went there from October through June, and that is where Jonathan finished his high-school saga. It had taken him four years and four different high schools, but he had done it. I, of course, attended his graduation ceremony with pride.

It turned out, however, that Jonathan had been right. Pretty much about everything. All he had needed was one very good audition. He got it and, as a result, he got into one of the finest conservatories in the country. As a student there he was allowed to take academic classes at the university across town, so he wound up getting the liberal arts education I had always wanted for him. He studied math seriously, learned foreign languages, and read good literature. Years after he completed his conservatory training and his university studies, he let me in on a little secret: the document they had handed him at that high-school graduation ceremony years ago was not a high-school diploma. It simply read: "Certificate of Attendance."

But by then I could laugh, because Jonathan was already well on his way to becoming the classical musician he wanted to be. He would have his career, even without a high-school diploma.

Sometimes, as a parent, you teach your children what will work best for them. Sometimes your children teach you.

CHAPTER TWO

FIRST SIGNS OF TALENT

Musical genius can announce itself when children are absurdly young. In the film *Amadeus,* we were treated to the story of three-year-old Mozart, who stunned the European royal courts with musical miracles. Mozart's legendary precociousness is in a class by itself, but many other musicians also displayed enormous talents in their childhood.

What is less known, however, and surely more surprising, is that many youngsters who grew up to be brilliant composers and performers showed little musical promise in their youth. Their childhoods were blatantly average.

This is what Peter Ilyich Tchaikovsky's biographer wrote about Tchaikovsky as a five-year-old:

The Pleasures and Perils of Raising Young Musicians

> It is commonplace at this early point in the biographies of composers to paint a picture of the young genius at the piano night and day, eschewing the outdoor games of his contemporaries, preferring to sight-read symphonies and pick out fledgling melodies before his feet can even reach the pedals. If Tchaikovsky is an exception, it is only insofar as he displayed no outstanding talent at this age.[1]

Nor did Richard Wagner impress his family or friends with any particular talent. As an adult reflecting on his childhood, Wagner wrote that his mother had "noticed nothing in me that might suggest a talent for music." [2] Likewise, when the great Italian opera composer Giacomo Puccini was young, he was said to be taciturn and to have no interest in music (or in much else, for that matter). As his biographer tells it,

> There was a piano in the room, but the young boy had little inclination to go near it. He had little inclination to do anything in particular...His purpose in school was the age-old purpose of the average boy, that is, to learn as little as possible and to get through with it. [3]

That does not sound like a promising start for the life of a musician who would go on to compose some of the most dramatic opera the world has known. The biographer's description sounds more like a complaint of one of today's concerned parents.

A story is told about the great Italian tenor Enrico Caruso who did have an early enthusiasm for singing: "As a child it was his chore to bring mozzarella to the village doctor's house and, after he left his delivery in the kitchen, he would listen furtively behind a closed door to Amelia, the doctor's daughter, as she gave singing lessons." [4]

In a gentle mockery of this *wunderkind* phenomenon, Shostakovich, the 20th century Russian composer, wrote in his autobiography: "I didn't sneak to the door at the age of three in order to listen to music, and when I did listen to it, I slept afterward just as soundly as the night before." [5]

Chapter Two: First Signs Of Talent

Similarly, Vladimir Horowitz, the astonishingly gifted Russian-American pianist, impressed no one when he was a child. This is how Horowitz the child was described:

> He barely touched the piano at age six and was certainly not considered a *wunderkind*. In fact, during the boy's first two years of lessons, his parents viewed him merely as somewhat above average….there was no evidence that anything extraordinary would develop, not the slightest hint that their son would one day be hailed as the king of piano virtuosos, the most charismatic performer since Franz Liszt.[6]

Nor did Sergei Prokofiev, the Russian composer, show any early promise.

> It was only when he entered the Conservatory, at age thirteen, that he began to demonstrate his exceptional natural gifts to their full extent…He did not compose symphonies before learning to walk. He did not even learn to play the piano until he was almost six, and did not master it in any significant sense until his adolescent years.[7]

- **Musical Precocity**

We don't often hear stories about great musicians growing up with an absence of obvious talent. But the child who exhibits unusual ability from an early age holds a certain fascination and provides us with the stuff of legends. Stories of child prodigies intrigue us because they imply a mystical quality as if these children come into our world pre-programmed to become musicians.

A prodigy is "a child with a rare and precocious ability to execute technically advanced pieces of music with an expressiveness that would seem beyond their years." However, "prodigy" is a politically incorrect term today, especially in the United States where we are very concerned with egalitarianism. Our culture is uncomfortable with the idea that some children are born with greater gifts than others, especially since, in the United States, prodigies tend to emerge from a few overachieving immigrant groups. A generation ago a wave of Jewish prodigies included Yehudi Menuhin, Itzhak Perlman and

Jascha Heifetz. Today the majority, like Sarah Chang and Midori, are Asian-born or the children of recent Asian immigrants.

In our culture, many people believe that prodigies are mentally ill victims of controlling, over-ambitious parents who are robbing their child of the "right" kind of childhood. There are cases like this, of course, but most often it is not the parents who are setting the agenda, but their children. Most parents simply want their children to be happy. When criticized for not living a normal childhood, Sarah Chang sniffed, "Well, I'd rather practice and do all this traveling than sit in front of the television four hours a day, which is what everyone does in this country."

Children who are gifted musically frequently display their ability at a very young age, but this is often not the case with painters or novelists, whose talents are usually appreciated much later in life. The only other field in which brilliance is displayed so early is mathematics, and there are many theories to explain how math and music talents are related. But what is it about music that makes it manifest itself in a child at the age of two or three?

Schopenhauer claimed that the early emergence of musical talent proved that music was the most basic of the arts: since we can respond to music without rational thought, experience, or language, we don't require age or education to comprehend and demonstrate musicality. George Marek suggests that:

> the explanation lies obviously in the nature of music itself, the art having the least connection with the outside world, the art which resides entirely in imagination and is disassociated from "real" life, that life for the grasping of which some measure of experience and maturity is required…That is not to suggest that music is freed of the requirement of reasoning, contemplation, growth in craftsmanship; it is merely to suggest that the experience of living is not the spark which ignites the fire.[8]

The "fire" of music seems to be inborn and sensitivity to music can express itself even before birth. This is what I, myself, experienced.

Chapter Two: First Signs Of Talent

When I was nine-months and uncomfortably pregnant with my son, I was taken to a wonderful concert, but I was distracted from the drama of the music by the drama in my body. I was getting an internal pounding, in perfect sync with the pounding from the stage. It was a lively evening. The morning after, when the drumming died down, I gave birth to Jonathan, joking that he would grow up to be a percussionist.

I'm not the only one to have that experience. Late in her pregnancy a Florida woman became alarmed when she sensed that her baby had not moved for a long time. But when she went to church that Sunday and the organ started up, the baby came back to life, kicking in time with the rhythm. The woman gave birth later that night to a girl who grew up to be a professional harpist.

These anecdotes suggest that even before birth, children display a connection to music.

Ten Early Signs of Musical Talent

- **# 1: Early Fascination with Music**

Not surprisingly, this early love of music is a common motif in children who grew up to be musicians. I remember taking my family downtown on Saturday mornings to hear the Los Angeles Philharmonic perform children's concerts where my son Jonathan, then only two, would sit transfixed. Other parents remember that their young children would listen to music on the radio and would cry when the station was changed.

In his autobiography, Aaron Copland remembers the old phonograph in his cousins' house in the Bronx where, he said, "I would sit for hours with my ear to the horn listening to popular records." [9]

The parents of Jose Carreras, one of the popular "three tenors," recalled that when their son was six, the family purchased a record player and little Jose was fascinated by a recording of the soundtrack from the film, "*The Great Caruso*," sung by Mario Lanza. They said that he "played it over and over...and from this moment on," they said, "there was always someone singing in the Carreras home" and it wasn't only Mario Lanza.[10]

The popular composer George Gershwin had a powerful childhood memory of being mesmerized by a particular piece of music:

> One of my first definite memories goes back to the age of six. I stood outside a penny arcade listening to an automatic piano leaping through Rubinstein's Melody in F. The peculiar jumps in the music held me rooted. To this very day I can't hear the tune without picturing myself outside that arcade on One Hundred and Twenty-fifth Street, standing there barefoot and in overalls, drinking it all in avidly.[11]

Parents are frequently startled by their infant's strong musical preference and only later realize that this is indicative of the child's musical sensitivity. The mother of Richard Strauss, the German composer, said that "from his earliest childhood, he smiled at the sound of the horn and cried loudly when he heard the violin."[12] The fact that his father played the horn no doubt had something to do with the child's preference.

The renowned violinist, Yehudi Menuhin, said that when he was three-years old, sitting on a parent's knee at a symphony concert in San Francisco's Curran Theater, he waited for the "sweet lovely sound of the violin floating up to the gallery," and his father confirmed that when he took his young son to concerts, Yehudi was entranced by the violin.[13] As we will later note, musical children are often drawn to a particular instrument.

- **# 2: Singing**

Song is the most natural way we humans make music, and the most common way a child's talent makes itself known is through singing. Singing was the first indication of my son's musical aptitude. On Friday nights our family gathered around the table to welcome the Jewish Sabbath, eat, and sing traditional blessings. One Friday night,

Chapter Two: First Signs Of Talent

when Jonathan was nine months old, I moved his high chair into the dining room in preparation for the evening's festive meal, and he began to sing. The words were incoherent, but the melody was clear and correct. I stood dumbfounded. This child—who had not yet begun to walk or to speak—was singing the melody of the traditional blessing over the wine! We found it funny, amazing, and more than a little wonderful. It can take a 13-year-old boy months to master this blessing for his Bar Mitzvah.

Other parents of musicians report that their children hummed tunes in infancy. One California child, at 11 months, would hum an Elvis song, "Bless My Soul," and come in with an "uh" right on cue. Today he is a composer. A six-year-old Florida girl, who would become a fine harpist, sang so well that she was asked by a local adult singing group to join them. When the adults forgot their parts, this child would sing the correct part for them; they used her as a little prop when they got lost and needed some help.

Pablo Casals, the Spanish cellist, came from a musical family and his father was a music pedagogue. Nevertheless, his early ability to sing amazed his parents. His biographer notes that Casals'

> aural response was such that he could sing in tune before he could speak. Before he could walk, [his mother] brought him downstairs one day and interrupted her husband's singing class...the infant had been reproducing accurately a progression [his father] was demonstrating. The father played a scale, Pablo repeated his performance, and the young members of the class went home to report that Carlos Casals' baby already knew solfeggio [the art of singing the names of the notes].[14]

The father of Franz Liszt, himself a pianist, first knew of his son's genius from the child's ability to remember and sing back what he had heard. As the father writes,

> In his sixth year [Franz] heard me play Ries's Concerto in C-sharp minor. Franz, bending over the piano, was completely absorbed. In the evening, coming in from a short walk in the garden, he sang the theme of the concerto! We made him sing

it again. He did not know what he was singing. That was the first indication of his genius.[15]

Gustav Mahler, the Austrian composer and conductor, recalled several scenes from his youngest days:

> Apparently I was still a babe in arms when I copied little songs and sang them back. Then, when I must have been about three, I was given an accordion and by working out the notes of the things I had heard I was soon able to play them perfectly.

> One day when I was not yet four a funny thing happened. A military band—something I delighted in all my childhood—came marching past our house one morning. I no sooner heard it than I shot out of the living room. Wearing scarcely more than a chemise—they hadn't dressed me yet—I trailed after the soldiers with my little accordion until quite some time later a couple of ladies from near by discovered me at the market place. [16]

The classical composer Robert Schumann had a very poor academic record in first grade, but his parents thought he might not be untalented in everything. They decided to give him piano lessons because, as they explained, he "sang a great deal." His singing saved him.

- **# 3: Rhythm**

Very young children who turn out to have a special feel for music often display a fondness for rhythmic language, the words of songs, or poetry. As a toddler, my son was totally uninterested in the standard children's story books that so captivated his older siblings, but wanted to hear nursery rhymes from the *Random House Book of Children's Verse*. He adored Shel Silverstein poems. He would sit still as long as we were reading something with a rhythmic beat. As babies, many musical children like silly chants with strong rhythmic elements. They read the words to songs over and over, relishing the rhythms and giggling over the rhymes.

Chapter Two: First Signs Of Talent

- **# 4: Toy Instruments and Make-Believe**

Children who grow up with musical instruments in the house are naturally inclined to explore them. But children without the real thing can communicate their interest by playing with toy instruments. One contemporary parent remembers it this way:

> my toddler was always pounding on the "play" drums that Santa brought him or walking around with a little plastic guitar and sun glasses pretending that he was Elvis. He liked to make musical noises, so we thought maybe we should give him lessons.

The mother of a Kentucky violinist laughed when her three-year-old son "conducted" the family as if they were an orchestra. She said,

> One day, he cleared everything off of the kitchen table, opened a book on it, tapped a pencil, said, "It's music time" and proceeded to direct us. He conducted all around the house to everything he heard. He would put a little suit on, stand in front of his brother and sister and try to conduct them. It was funny, but he took it all so seriously, you know. I guess that's just a musician.

She was bemused then and is now by his utter seriousness. Though she is still mystified today, she is willing to go along with it, especially since she sees how much he loves his violin.

Tchaikovsky was obsessed, as a child, with fingering tunes on whatever surface he could find. "An over-vigorous exercise of this practice on a window led to a broken pane and a badly cut hand, and it was this incident that persuaded his parents to take his musical inclinations seriously" [17] and hire a piano teacher for him.

It usually doesn't require such high drama to get the attention of parents today.

- **# 5: Gentle Touch on the Piano**

Singing "on key," enjoying rhythmic verse, playing with toy instruments, and "conducting" the family are easily recognizable signs of musical interest. But there are other, not so obvious, indications of talent.

Most toddlers, seeing a piano keyboard, love to finger it. Most of them enjoy "banging" happily on the keys and setting everyone's teeth on edge. As a two-year old, my son Jonathan would climb up on the piano bench like all the other two-year olds but, unlike most of his age mates, he did not bang on the keys. He fingered them very gently. I thought he was simply inhibited, but I later learned that this is a well recognized sign of musical aptitude.

Jacqueline's mother tells a parallel story. When Jacqueline, a New Yorker who later became an opera singer, first went to pre-school, she ignored the other children in order to spend time on the piano she found there. Jacqueline was the only pre-school child allowed to play the teacher's piano because she didn't bang on it like the others. She would play it very softly, looking for hidden tunes.

The mother of Van Cliburn, the Texas piano *wunderkind*, noted this behavior in her young son:

> What really impressed me in Van's earliest years was the way he would touch the keyboard, before he could walk or talk. Most children, seeing the keys of a piano for the first time, instinctively bang upon them with all their might, expressing the universal human desire to make a noise. But when I held little Van over the keyboard he leaned down and touched one key at a time, very gently. This gave me my first indication of his true musicality. [18]

Glenn Gould's father reported similar restraint in his son's behavior:

> As soon as Glenn was old enough to be held on his grandmother's knee at the piano, he would never pound the keyboard as most children will with the whole hand, striking a number of keys at a time, instead he would always insist on pressing down a single key and holding it down until the resulting sound had completely died away. [19]

Chapter Two: First Signs Of Talent

- **# 6: Playing Tunes**

A sure sign of musical talent is a young child's ability to hear a melody and then to *play* it on the piano. Darius Milhaud, the French composer, told how his mother discovered his musical ability.

> Mother told me that she heard someone playing "Funiculi, funicular" on the old piano in the drawing-room. She thought it was my grandmother, who occasionally amused herself by picking out old tunes, but she could not understand where [grandmother] had learnt that particular melody, nor why she was playing it so hesitantly. So [mother] went into the drawing-room to clear up the mystery, and found me all alone perched on a stool and absorbed in groping after the tune I had heard some little Italians singing under our window a few weeks before.[20]

Marian Filar told how his family discovered his musical talent when he was five, and how this led to his getting music lessons.

> When we returned home to Warsaw after six weeks at Ciechocinek [a spa town where concerts were regularly played], I went straight to our upright piano and picked out with one finger most of the beautiful themes from Mozart, Beethoven, and Tchaikovsky that I had heard at the concerts. As you can imagine, this caused quite a sensation among the family members. So my mother arranged to bring me to see Josef Goldberg, a well-known teacher of gifted children with special musical talent.[21]

Richard Rogers, the Broadway composer, writes not about his parents' discovery of his talent, but of his own discovery. He found that he was able to reproduce on the piano the "beautiful sounds" that he had heard his mother make.

> I don't know exactly how old I was when I first tried to play the piano, but I gather that I had to be lifted onto the piano stool. I had heard all those beautiful sounds my mother could make simply by pressing her fingers down on the keys, and I wanted more than anything else to be able to make the same beautiful sounds. I wasn't much more than a toddler when I discovered that I was able to reproduce the melodies with accuracy.[22]

- **# 7: Reading Music**

Some children, at a very young age, are even able to read music. Glenn Gould could read music before he read words. Four-year old Yvonne, now on her way to being a professional violinist and pianist, was able to read music before she could read words. Her mother says, "No one ever taught her to read music, but she could do it. She must have picked it up herself, sitting on my lap when I took her older sister to Yamaha music classes."

The mother of Cameron explains how her daughter, at age three, learned to read music:

> At church, I always followed the words of the hymns with my fingers, thinking it might help my children learn to read the words, but one day I realized that Cameron was reading the notes instead of the words! She could point to the notes of any hymn and sing them!

- **# 8: Writing Music**

After reading, comes writing. And this is as true of music as it is of verbal language. Drawing and writing music-like shapes are other ways young children express their interest in music. Sometimes, like all two-year olds, Jonathan liked to scribble and call it drawing. Sometimes he drew faces, but often he drew black circles with straight lines protruding from them. Sometimes he drew five parallel lines, vaguely reminiscent of a staff and decorated it with black circles. I just laughed.

The governess of Sergei Prokofiev also laughed when she saw what six-year old Sergei had drawn, and what he expected of her.

> Sitting at a desk [Prokofiev] used to cover pages of paper with the musical signs he had seen. He drew notes and clefs as other children drew cats, ducks, or trains. Unfortunately, the collection of musical signs that he scrawled did not have any meaning. Once, according to [his governess]…, he brought her a whole page covered with these "music notes," and said, "Here, I have composed Liszt's rhapsody. Play it for me." [23]

Chapter Two: First Signs Of Talent

She could only laugh because his scribbled signs were neither Liszt's rhapsody nor were they music. But they were a clear indication of Prokofiev's musical interest and talent.

- **# 9: Identifying Instruments and Transposing Music**

Some children evince their unusual musical abilities at a very young age when they are able to easily identify instruments they hear on the radio. Or they may do something that highly intelligent adults can struggle years to master—for instance, transposing music from one key to another. One parent realized that her third-grade daughter had musical talent when "she was playing Scott Joplin rags for friends and she simply picked up her hands, moved to a different key, and played the piece again. She thought that was perfectly normal, but the adults in the room at the time were speechless."

- **# 10: Perfect Pitch**

Perhaps the most mysterious of all of these signs of musical intelligence is that of perfect pitch. More accurately termed "absolute pitch," this is the ability to identify a single note immediately and with unerring accuracy. A person with perfect pitch can tell instantly when a tone is a C rather than a B and, when asked to do so, can sing a tone, any tone, with utter ease. Most of us, adults as well as children, even after years of study and practice, are simply unable to accomplish this feat.

When Samantha had just turned three, her family moved from Massachusetts to Connecticut where they acquired an upright piano. Samantha's mother, Lily, sat down at the piano to plunk out a melody. She recalled this scene vividly:

> I don't really know how to play—we're not a musical family—but I could manage 'Do-Re-Mi,' from The Sound of Music." Samantha was delighted. A few days later, I was in the kitchen heating food in the microwave and it was humming. Samantha said, "It's a Do, Mommy!" I ran over to the piano and played that note. Sure enough it was a Do. My daughter knew instinctively what note my microwave hummed!" [24]

This is such a fascinating phenomenon that it deserves a short digression.

Perfect pitch is a rare occurrence: only one out of 10,000 Americans has it. To those of us without perfect pitch, the ability to hear and name a note seems uncanny, but those who have this foolproof ability say it is as obvious as identifying a color. In fact, people with perfect pitch often explain that they name a note in the same way that they name a color. Nicolas Slonimsky said, "I knew that E-flat was E-flat when struck on the piano when I was a small child, and I knew that it was as different from E-natural as red is from pink." [25] Perfect pitch is so natural to those who possess it, that they are surprised to learn that everyone else cannot hear what they hear. (As I was once surprised to learn that there are people in the world who cannot distinguish between red and green.) It is that obvious to them.

Most musicians, however, do not have perfect pitch. They have what is called "relative pitch," which is the ability to find a note if they are first given another note as a reference point. For instance, if you play a C, they can quickly hum you an F-sharp. Many musicians memorize one note and then use that note as a pole star for navigating and finding the others. But, unlike those with perfect pitch, it takes these musicians an instant to calculate and perform the navigation and frequently they are a bit off. Many musicians have a form of perfect pitch limited to their own instrument. A pianist, for example, may be able to easily identify a G on the piano, but not on any other instrument.

Certainly, having perfect pitch attests to a child's musical talent. But the absence of perfect pitch does not indicate inferior musical ability. In fact, many of the finest musicians and composers, including Tchaikovsky and Wagner, did not have perfect pitch.

Parents of children with perfect pitch may be puzzled by their child's peculiar ability to hear what they, the parents, cannot. Many parents ask their child how they know what they know, but these children are unable to explain how they know an F from an E. They are

Chapter Two: First Signs Of Talent

simply giving names to what they hear. The father of a Nebraska boy says,

> My son will be listening to something in the car and, I don't know where this came from, but he will say, "That's in G Major."
>
> And I say, "It is? How do you know that?"
>
> And he says, "I just know."

Perfect pitch is so accurate that its use can create an experience of shock to people who don't have it. Marian Filar tells how his parents reacted to this eye-opening incident:

> To try out my musical ear, Mr. Goldberg played a ten-note chord using both hands and asked me to tell him what the notes were. I immediately gave my answer, but my mother, who had seen his hands and the piano keys he had pressed, said, "Oh, that's wrong," believing I was off by a half tone.
>
> "No, it *is* a half tone lower, Mrs. Filar," Mr. Goldberg said. "He's dead right. My piano is badly out of tune. He has perfect pitch."
>
> That news convinced my parents that I should begin musical studies.[26]

Today new research suggests that perfect pitch is more common than it seems and that, like second languages, it can be learned. This view is supported by the fact that in spoken languages where pitch is used to convey meaning (like Chinese or Vietnamese) perfect pitch occurs more commonly. Because of this, researchers have suggested that infants have better pitch perception than adults but may lose this capacity unless they use it for learning tonal languages.

The absence of perfect pitch in no way indicates a child's inferior musical ability. However, if your child has the phenomenon of perfect pitch, she is clearly demonstrating unusual musical aptitude.

- **What To Do About Early Musical Interest or Ability**

Demonstrating the phenomenon of perfect pitch, being able to recall a tune, or simply approaching the piano keyboard gently, all indicate a musical sensitivity or talent or genius—pick your term. If your child exhibits any of these qualities, it is safe to assume that he or she has pronounced musical ability. Most children have greater ability than is generally recognized, but today there are too few opportunities for displaying and recognizing musical talent. It is crucial to realize, however, that children who display none of the above behaviors may have the same, untapped capabilities.

So what's the best course of action for a parent? Expose your children to all kinds of music. Sing to them. Dance with them. Take them to concerts. Get them the best music education you can afford. And enjoy together all the music you hear, make, discover, and explore.

CHAPTER THREE

YOU WANT TO PLAY THE *WHAT?* HOW CHILDREN CHOOSE INSTRUMENTS

Many children (both famous musicians of yesterday and also today's eight-year olds) select the instrument they want to play with a strong degree of certainty. Why do they want to play one instrument and not another? Some children know why they made their selection. For others, and especially for their parents, the choice remains a mystery. Nevertheless, when a child is determined to play a particular instrument, it is best to follow his lead, as this is usually the "right" instrument for that child. This chapter offers many examples of this phenomenon.

We will begin by looking at the piano—why it is chosen and why it is not. It can be challenging at first to see beyond the piano as the perfect option, since in the United States pianos are almost universally available.

We will continue by looking at how other instruments are selected, mostly from the child's point of view. We will look further at instrument choice in the next chapter, this time from the perspective of the parent who is making the choice or is helping her child to make the choice.

- **Why the Piano?**

It's easy to see why most people choose the piano for their child's first music lessons. Pianos are ubiquitous and versatile. They are seen in schools and on television, in seedy bars and in classy department stores. They make fiery solo instruments and subdued accompaniment for soloists. Because pianos are everywhere, you will hear few stories from parents about how their child "discovered" the piano.

Pianos are found in many homes, even where no instrument is played. Families inherit pianos. They might feel that a piano looks elegant in a living room, giving off the whiff of culture. A piano may be used as a personal statement, whether artsy or decorative. Someone in the family might have played it as a child and long after the child left home, the piano remained. Or a parent might plan to offer the children music lessons one day. Parents may hope to give *themselves* music lessons one day. They may believe that the piano is the easiest instrument to play.

Comparing the piano to, say, an oboe, even a novice would know how to begin playing it: you just press those keys and out come tones. The keys, and the tones they produce, are arranged in disarmingly simple fashion. Arrayed from the lowest note on the far left to the highest note on the far right, the notes lie in perfect sequence. This is certainly not the case with string or wind instruments.

The piano invites touch, touch begets sound, and a child can pick out simple melodies. In addition, the piano is capable of producing multiple tones, making satisfying harmonies and providing its own accompaniment. It takes only two fingers on two keys to produce a pleasing harmony, and when eight fingers hit eight different keys, the effect of the piano can be dazzling.

A practical advantage of pianos is that they are relatively easy to maintain. A weekly dusting and yearly tuning will suffice to keep a piano in excellent condition, whereas orchestral instruments can fail suddenly in ways that are highly technical, expensive, and confusing.

It is also easy to find a piano teacher. There are organizations of music teachers in every city as well as several national organizations for piano teachers. Piano recitals are frequent, and piano competitions, common.

Nor is it difficult to purchase or rent a piano, since the piano industry is well oiled, piano stores are convenient, and pianos are easily accessible. Piano stores sell music and often provide references for teachers and piano tuners.

In addition to all these advantages, the piano has a rich and extensive repertoire. Virtually every great composer has written music for the piano. There are piano pieces for every taste and performance level, from grade-school easy to diabolically difficult. There are great numbers of solos, duets, chamber music, and concertos. Some composers, notably Chopin, wrote almost exclusively for the piano. Although there is a sizable literature of solo works for other instruments, the piano repertoire stands alone in its richness.

- **Why Not the Piano?**

With all the advantages that the piano offers, why would any child begin his or her musical studies on an instrument other than the piano? Well, one answer is this: the overwhelming majority of children who study piano quit—some sooner, some later.

Why is this so?

The piano, although it looks simple to play, is actually quite difficult to master. Because its range of 88 notes is so large, the piano requires two staffs, the top treble clef and the bottom bass clef. Each staff looks the same but is played differently. Only the clef sign at the beginning of each line identifies the clef. A note written on the first rung of the treble clef is E above middle C, but that same symbol on the same line of the bass clef is a low G. Mastering this complexity is not trivial.

In contrast to the pianist's formidable challenge, wind and string instrument players read only one clef and play only one note at a time. To be sure, there are celebrated passages, especially in the violin repertoire, which require "double stops," or two-note chords. But for the most part all orchestral players can concentrate on playing a single note at a time.

Not only must the pianist read different notes on different staffs, but these notes often have different values (lengths) or rhythms, and the player must read and perform all these different notes and rhythms at the same time! He or she must watch two hands that are doing different things in different directions, simultaneously, and this is not easy.

The reason so many piano students quit piano, however, is not because of the piano's technical challenges. It's because they don't get a payoff. The payoff I'm referring to comes from group performances. Pianists either perform at home for family and friends or in an occasional recital, and they seldom play with others, whereas orchestral instruments are "made" for playing together in groups. Chamber music, for instance, requires a small number of usually different instruments. Each instrument has a unique musical voice and an essential role in making the music. No instrument can "hide" inside a section of similar instruments, which means that each instrument and each performer is heard and uniquely appreciated. Children enjoy playing together, whether the play is sports, make-believe, or making music. When they have the opportunity to play together in chamber groups or in an orchestra, they experience the pleasure of making real music (and often of making real friends). They tell jokes, share "mess-ups," and generally have a good time. If they don't stay with their instruments for the sake of the music, they may stay with them for the sake of their friends.

- **Found Instruments**

It's easy to understand why and how people start to study the piano. But how does a child start on a bassoon, or a violin for that matter?

Sometimes a child selects an instrument and plays it for many years because, like the piano, the instrument happens to be in the house or in the family. Here are three examples: Kassie, a high-school violinist in Utah, was in fourth grade when she discovered that her grandfather had played the violin when he was a boy and still had a couple of old, beat-up violins lying around. She convinced her parents to let her try one. Andrea, another high school student, took to the clarinet in fifth grade when she came across her mother's old instrument in the basement. Lauren found an old French horn in her grandmother's attic and played "with" it. Later she learned to play it.

- **Kids Who Know What They Want**

Many parents tell stories about how their child hounded them for a particular instrument. My son Jonathan was insistent from the very beginning about his choice of the flute. One father watched his five-year-old daughter "drive herself nuts trying to learn how to play the violin that we had at home." He said, "She refused to be parted from it and was pleading for some way to make the thing work. Finally we had to find her a teacher."

A California boy made a toy violin out of cardboard "with an F hole and everything." He made a bow out of Tinkertoys, and played "the violin" all over the house until his parents finally agreed to get him a real one. The father of Soovin Kim, an acclaimed young American violinist, recounts that by the age of four, his son was obsessed with the violin and walked around the house with a book tucked under his chin and a chopstick for his bow.

That is also how Joseph Haydn first displayed his musicality: when the five-year-old Haydn sat listening to his first concert, he "sawed at his left arm with a stick," to mimic the violins.[27] Evidently he kept up the correct rhythm, because the conductor (who was the headmaster of a fine music school) was so impressed by the boy that he convinced Haydn's parents to send him to Hainburg where Haydn got an education, not only in music, but also in reading, writing and religion.

In our own time, a four-year-old girl in Los Angeles was taken by her mother to a "Mommy and Me" piano class. Later, when mother and daughter went to a music store to buy a metronome for her piano practice, the child pointed to a small violin and said, "I want to play that guitar." Her mother, always in a hurry, hushed her daughter and said, "That's not a guitar." The child was usually very reticent, but in the store she cried so vehemently that her mother had to drag her away. The next time they went in to the store to buy music for her piano class, the child pointed a second time at the small-size violin and said, "I want to play that little guitar." The mother again corrected her, saying, "That is not a guitar. That is a little violin." The daughter took the correction and replied, "OK. I want to play that little violin." Her mother gave up, gave in, and bought her daughter a small, $90, made-in-China violin. Her happy daughter eventually became a fine violinist, but the mother never did discover why her child was so irresistibly drawn to the violin.

One father told this story about his three-year-old daughter who insisted on "playing the rulers." She held two 12-inch rulers, pretending one was the violin and the other, the bow. But since there was already a violinist in the family, the parents thought their daughter should play a different instrument and they started her on the flute. Her parents and teacher spent three months trying to teach this young child how to blow on a flute by telling her to pretend she was "spitting rice." The girl was a good trouper and went along with it, although she kept asking, "But when do I get my violin?" Each day, after she had satisfactorily completed her flute exercise, she would ask, "Do I get my violin now?" It was as if all this flute business was simply an obstacle that she had to overcome. Finally, when the child was almost four years old, her parents gave in and got her a violin.

Violinists are not the only young musicians expressing such dogged determination. One Pittsburgh mother was baffled by her son's insistence on the trumpet. Jon had been asking for music lessons from the time he was in first grade. His mother began searching for someone to advise her. She was sent to the band directors who taught the upper classes at her son's school. They agreed to evaluate Jon to see if he could take up an instrument at such a young age. The band directors looked him over and examined his teeth, noting that Jon would need braces and so would not be a good candidate for a brass instrument. They recommended the clarinet or drums. But Jon said no. The only instrument he wanted to play was the trumpet. The teachers tried to discourage him, but the child insisted. His mother finally rented a trumpet and Jon continued playing his trumpet for 12 years, through braces and other formidable obstacles, never wavering from his initial choice.

- **A Child's Sense of Musical Identity**

Some children have such a strong sense of identity with their instrument that it mystifies their parents, although eventually they come to accept it. The memory of the day my seven-year-old son saw and selected the flute from all the instruments that were on display— with certainty, passion, and urgency— has never faded from my memory. Here are two examples of parents who were similarly surprised by their children's intense sense of personal identity.

A mother in Atlanta recalled that it was always something of an ordeal to get her daughter's cello into the car for her weekly cello lesson. The trunk of the car was not quite big enough, so they maneuvered the cello in and out of the back seat. The mother would say to her daughter, "Aren't you sorry you don't play the flute or the violin?" And her daughter would invariably reply, with that air of exasperation children save for their Neanderthal parents, "Mother, I play the *cello!*" The child's sense of musical identity was perfectly clear.

A mother in Connecticut recalled her son Craig's problems the summer that his friends began to play soccer seriously. Her son was not at all interested in sports, but he was interested in having friends, so this mother decided to send her son Craig to a summer music camp.

> He took his guitar to camp but while there, became fascinated by the orchestra and, in particular, the tuba. I tried to get him interested in the trombone instead since its mouthpiece and range are similar to that of the tuba's. I felt the trombone would offer him a greater range of possibilities. But he resisted fiercely. When he came home from camp he immediately started calling every music store in Connecticut to find a tuba. To make matters worse (certainly to make them more expensive), you can't *rent* tubas in Connecticut; it seems you can only *buy* them. Craig had never yet tried to *play* a tuba and yet here he was, a 13-year old, trying to *buy* one. He succeeded. He got his tuba—winning the battle with me as well as the opportunity to play tuba in some excellent orchestras all the way to the conservatory. Years later I asked him why he had been so resistant to the trombone. He was puzzled by my obtuseness, saying, "But Mother, I'm a valve person, not a slide person!"

He knew exactly who he was and was taken aback when he discovered that she did not.

- **The Influence of Other Children**

A primary way children learn is through imitation. Children learn from one another effortlessly, imitating what they see and hear.

This is a common reason for a child's wanting to play a particular instrument: his friend is doing it. A California grandmother was raising her grandson, Cameron. His kindergarten friend brought to school a violin for "Show and Tell" and, from that day, Cameron wanted one, too.

Chapter Three: You Want To Play The What?

A girl in Florida saw a child in a music store taking a lesson on a lap harp and told her parents she wanted to play it, but they paid little attention. Later she convinced her father to go back to the store and get the harp— for her mother's birthday. Like the boy who gets his mother a puppy for Christmas, everyone knew just who the harp was for. The girl then persuaded her parents to give her harp lessons and is today a professional harpist.

In his autobiography, *My First 79 Years*, Isaac Stern wrote about how he decided he wanted to play the violin:

> I've often said that I didn't return home from a concert one day and plead for a violin. Nor did I begin, at the age of five or six, to pick out melodies on the piano. None of that; nothing so mysterious, so romantic. My friend Nathan Koblick was playing the violin; therefore I wanted to play the violin.[28]

Stern was clear about what he wanted and knew exactly why he wanted it.

- **The Influence of Parents and Siblings**

Jean-Pierre Rampal became a flutist because of his father, who was a famous flute teacher. Since children imitate their idols, many children will want to play what daddy or mommy plays. In his autobiography, *Music, My Love*, Rampal wrote,

> There was no doubt about which instrument I wanted to play...I worshiped my father and loved to hear and watch him play the flute...He had a sonority, a sound, that was very special, very much his own, very "fleshy" and full of emotion. You could not listen to him play without being intensely aware of it.[29]

Similarly, Daniel Barenboim tells that his earliest desire to play the piano was so that he could play with his father:

> When I was about four, my father gave some concerts with a violinist for which they used to rehearse at our flat. I suddenly wanted to play the violin, so that I could play with my father. I was rather small, and by the time my parents started looking

> for a violin that was the right size, I had seen my father playing duets with somebody on two pianos. Realizing that I, too, could play the piano with my father, I settled for that instead. I was five years old when I started.[30]

Children often want to play the instrument their older brother or sister played. As babies, younger siblings may mimic their older brother or sister on toys or makeshift instruments. There can be problems when two siblings play the same instrument, since the older one will usually be at a developmental advantage, and this can discourage the younger sibling. Kevin wanted to study the piano because his older sister did, but as a beginner he was very frustrated. He would ask, "How come Yvonne can play such nice pieces, and my pieces are so boring?" He constantly compared himself to his older sister and was constantly discouraged. His mother finally said, "OK. Why don't you play another instrument that Yvonne doesn't play?" And that's how Kevin started on the violin. He loved it and is today a performing violinist.

Many children, like Kevin, found their way to their particular instrument because it was *not* what their older sibling played. One California family started their daughter on cello in order to keep her away from her older brother's valuable violin. A Maryland boy whose older brother played the violin chose the viola to avoid competing with his always-in-the-limelight brother. A Florida bassist chose his instrument because his sisters had already cornered the violin, viola, and cello.

- **The Influence of Television**

Often children ask for an instrument that they see being played on television. Many children decided on the violin after seeing Itzhak Perlman on *Sesame Street*. Other children have asked for a cello "to be like Yo-Yo Ma." Often parents don't know where or when their child saw Perlman or Ma, but it is clear that these men have influenced the latest generation of young musicians raised in the age of television.

Chapter Three: You Want To Play The What?

- **Bonding with an Instrument**

It is not unusual to find that a child has developed an intense bond with his or her instrument. This phenomenon took place in my living room when my son Jonathan was given his first flute. The entire family gathered in our living room the night his teacher-to-be presented him with his beginner's instrument. It was a night we would long remember, because of his excitement. His eyes were fixed on the new black case and he itched to open the clasps that help it closed. When he opened the case, his teacher showed him how to put the sections of the flute together and how to blow over the hole in the mouthpiece to get a sound. Jonathan was enchanted when he found he could get it to whistle for him. It was love at first sight.

Parents all across the country can recall a moment when they recognized that an intense bonding was taking place between their child and a new instrument.

A San Francisco mother reported that when her son got his first oboe, he was "holding it in his lap in the back seat of the car on the way home, like it was his baby. Just the way he was looking at it..." her voice trailed off, literally at a loss for words. The mother of a drummer from Houston tells that when her son came home and said that he was going to play the drums, she thought,

> Well, this is as good as anything else a sixth grader could do, so I said, 'OK, Let's get you some sticks.' And from the moment he first held those mallets in his hands, he was in heaven.

The father of a Minneapolis violist said that his daughter had played the violin only half-heartedly. When she switched to the viola, however, she immediately learned the new clef, took immaculate care of her viola, and refused to be parted from it.

The parent of a bassist from Louisville, Kentucky, described her daughter as being hooked by music only after she switched instruments. "When she gave up the violin for the bass she just blossomed. She talked about her bass non-stop, about how it was different, about how she didn't care that it was different. It was special, and it made her feel special."

There seems to be a certain mystique about the string bass. There aren't all that many classical bass players. One Florida cellist hungered to play the bass. The fact that his school had no bass for him to play made it seem all the more exotic. From fourth grade on, he played the cello, but it was only when he went to middle school and found a real bass that he made real musical progress because he had "found" his instrument. "It made him feel important to play the bass. It's big. People notice. Playing the bass meant he was somebody," said his mother.

- **The Personal Fit**

Some people speak of a spiritual or personal "fit" between the instrument and the player. The mother of a harpist admits: "It sounds stupid to say it, but the harp is so angelic that it suits her. She really is a sweet kid." The father of a trombonist explained, "The trombone matches Madeleine's personality. She has an unusual character. She's got a lot of substance and she can stand up well to a group of guys. Plus, she likes to be different. So the trombone was the instrument for her!"

A cello teacher, impressed with Chris, her new student, asked, "Did your first teacher teach you that? No? Then you must have been a cellist in another life." Chris' mother felt that, indeed, Chris' attachment to his cello was so unique that only a spiritual connection could explain it.

- **Size Matters**

More often the "fit" is a physical fit—an instrument has to be the right size for the person who plays it. The biographer of the legendary clarinetist, Benny Goodman, writes that Benny's father was the person who consciously fit him and his two brothers with their first instruments.

Chapter Three: You Want To Play The What?

> Pop took Harry, Freddy, and Benny...to the synagogue, where they were fitted out with instruments...Harry was given a tuba because he was the biggest, Freddy a trumpet because he was next in size and Benny the clarinet, because he was the smallest.[31]

This "Three Little Bears" approach was used as well by a trombonist from Gainesville, Florida, who said,

> I tried out the trumpet and it just seemed very small. It was the same thing with the French horn—too small and uncomfortable. I also tried out the tuba and it was like sticking my face in a sink to play, that's how big it felt. And then I tried the trombone and the trombone mouthpiece felt like just the right size. It rested comfortably on my lips and I was real satisfied playing it.

With the strings there can be a similar pattern. The teacher of a violist in New York told him that, since he was more than six feet tall, he would be better suited to the viola than the violin that he had been playing. A University of Michigan bassist started playing the bass after an elementary school teacher noted that the girl's height suggested the bass would be a good fit. Once this girl found the "right" instrument, she took to it with real gusto.

In describing her son's childhood, Marina Ma, mother of Yo-Yo, tells that he

> [had] no real interest in playing the violin, although he was very good at it...
>
> Yo-Yo said..."I don't like the sound violins make; I want a big instrument."
>
> Patiently, his father, Dr. Ma, improvised a "big instrument" by attaching an "end pin" to a viola. After all, that should satisfy a three-year old. So he thought. But Yo-Yo knew better and proved it at the Conservatory concert he attended with his father.

> Yo-Yo sat completely absorbed in what he heard, but especially in what he saw. "I want that," he told his father, jumping from his seat as he pointed to a big double-bass on the stage.
>
> "You don't want *that*; it's too big for you. You won't be able to hold it."
>
> Yo-Yo avoided the issue. He knew exactly what he wanted and was bent on getting it.[32]

His father relented and replaced his son's violin with a 1/16-size cello.

- **A Physical Fit**

Explanations given by young musicians for their choice of instrument reveal a whimsical, if visceral quality. A young violist told her father that the way the viola fit her hand "made my body feel good." When a mother asked her son Jarrod why he had chosen the trumpet, he laughed and said, "My body told me." He quickly ran outside to play with his brother and his mother shrugged.

This theme is echoed by the girl who told her mother she was going to play the cello because the "orchestra director told me that I have cello hands," and by the girl whose band teacher told her mother that "this kid's embouchure fits the French horn perfectly." ("Embouchure" is music-speak for the lips and their fine musculature.) One Kentucky mother, herself a musician, described the process she used to select the trombone for her daughter.

> I analyzed her mouth and her embouchure to see what would fit her. She has a little bit of a lip in the front. I took a flute and put it in the refrigerator and let it freeze up and I stuck it in front of her mouth. When she blew over it we both could see how her breath split the air, so I knew she couldn't play the flute. And you can't play a trumpet or a single reed instrument with that split air either. So I tried a double reed—an oboe reed. As soon as she tried it, she broke it, so that one was out. Her lips are a little bit bigger than usual, and the best instrument for her would probably be a tuba, but I didn't want

Chapter Three: You Want To Play The What?

her to march with a heavy tuba, so that was out too. So...by the process of elimination, we settled on the trombone.

An Omaha bassist explained that she had started on the violin, but she got tired holding it up all the time. She noticed that the cellos and basses were "all relaxed" since they could rest their arms on their instruments. She turned in her viola for a string bass and became a relaxed and happy bassist. Another young girl from Southern California complained that wind players like her older brothers couldn't chew and play at the same time, but that string players could, so she became a cellist.

A French horn player told me that she decided to continue with the horn because she was the only one in her orchestra who could perform for more than 20 minutes without getting dizzy. Dizziness is a common problem among young wind players, and many of them have to stop to rest before continuing to play. But an orchestra player can only rest when the music dictates a rest, so this can be a real problem for them.

- **Instruments as Physical Therapy**

Sometimes a parent selects an instrument to compensate for a weakness they perceive or to remedy a child's problem. A violinist from South Carolina explained that she was sickly and was hospitalized on several occasions when she was three years old. Her doctor recommended a sport or some other physical activity to improve her strength, but her mother decided to try the violin. The child started to play the violin, and she came to love it. She still plays the violin, and she is no longer troubled by weakness or fainting.

- **The Instrument's Sound**

Whereas many children respond to their instrument's physicality, others report that what hooked them on an instrument was the beautiful quality of its sound. Jacqueline du Pré's biographer described how the young du Pré announced her desire to play the cello:

> So it was that one day, while listening to a *Children's Hour* radio programme dedicated to instruments of the orchestra, Jackie first heard the sound of the cello. Without hesitation the four-year old declared to her mother, "That is the sound I want to make." [33]

It is this unhesitating quality that often makes a child's response seem so mysterious, as if it were pre-programmed. It is not an infrequent reaction. Here is Marian Filar's description of falling in love with the piano:

> The first time they handed [the violin] to me and I tried to play, I immediately started to cry and make a scene. I hated the thing. I couldn't find the right tone, the right key, or the right way to play on pitch. It drove me crazy. You never heard such a noise. That violin wailed and squeaked and screeched so much that it sounded like it was trying to scare all the mice out of the house. It was awful! I carried on and fussed, crying, "I don't wanna, I don't wanna." I made myself so obnoxious that they finally figured it wasn't worth it and switched me to the piano. Then I was happy. Life was all sunshine again. I had already fallen in love with the sound of the piano and that was what I wanted to play—the piano and only the piano. That has never changed." [34]

It is common for a child to express love for the sound of the piano, but what about the sound of the *channon?* When she was eight, Tami heard someone playing this 72-string Middle-Eastern instrument and fell in love with its sound. Years later, Tami went to UCLA, majored in music, and found someone there to teach her to play it.

The "Three Little Bears" theme—one too big, one too small, and one just right—applies to sound as well as size. A Louisville family listened in amazement as their son tried out the different string instruments. First he tried the cello: "Oh, no, the pitch is way too low." How about the violin? "Oh, no, the pitch is way too high." So we only had one string instrument in between, and that was the viola. There really was no decision. He tried it and said, "Yes, this sounds right. The pitch is just where it should be."

Chapter Three: You Want To Play The What?

There is one more choice in the string family, and that, of course, is the string bass. The sound of the bass was just right for a girl with a deep voice who lived in Washington, D.C. She loved the depth and seriousness of the bass and, though her ear was OK on other string instruments, only on the bass did she have perfect pitch.

A Korean mother tells the story of how she discovered her daughter's unusual talent for the French horn. In her own words:

> First time when Aria brought horn she was in sixth grade. School teacher calls me at 2:00. He kind of almost scream, "I cannot believe what your daughter did, it was amazing, she blew up to three scales." I couldn't understand what he said, so it sounds like to me, my interpretation was, "Oh, my God, this is Mozart in horn. And I call my husband, "You gotta come home, teacher call me, and he say it's so amazing, I couldn't believe." So my daughter comes home and I said, "What did you do?" And she said, "Mom, I don't know what I did. He told me push this button, push that button, so I pushed and then he called everybody around me and then I just played some notes. I don't know what I did." So then, next day, she come home with brand-new French horn. Teacher he was so excited he went to store that day and he bought horn and he give it to her next day. So I say, "OK, play for me what you did for teacher." And I'm thinking it's like beautiful melody, you know. Even after few measures, I think, OK, beauty part will soon come. But nothing. Like a gas passing. I say to her, "This is what you did? Yes?" So I see I need go to school and meet this teacher. I don't understand. I guess is because I'm so dumb in music.

Evidently, this daughter had a knack for the horn, because she loved it and continued to play it for many years.

Many young musicians report that they connected with their instrument when they found they could get a good sound out of it right from the beginning. That was true of my son Jonathan. The first time he tried, he surprised his teacher by getting a true tone out of his student flute. Another boy, Colin, remembers that, when he was five, he tried unsuccessfully to get a note out of the trumpet at a Pittsburgh Symphony Open House. But when he tried the strings, it was easy for him. Today Colin is a violist.

- **Selection Using the Suzuki Method**

There are many youngsters playing strings today because the well-regarded Suzuki music education programs teach these instruments. When her first-grade daughter was offered a little cello in her Orlando, Florida, public school's Suzuki program, one mother thought it was something of a joke and predicted that the girl's enthusiasm wouldn't last through Christmas. The parents agreed, however, to rent the little cello "and she's still playing today and she's 23 years old!"

Suzuki programs prefer the strings to the piano because string instruments can be scaled down to a child's size. Suzuki instructors believe that string instruments provide better ear training, and they like the fact that the strings require physical arm movement to sustain a note, giving the child kinesthetic validation and a strong foundation in note values.

- **Practical Motivations**

Stories of selecting an instrument because a child falls in love with the sound it makes (with its "voice," or "timbre," or "color"), or because that particular instrument speaks to the student in a uniquely personal way have a warm and sentimental feel. To better balance these feeling-based stories, we can look at practical motivations for selecting a specific instrument. Some people decide to play an instrument for economic, even mercenary reasons. Since some instruments are more difficult to master, they are played by fewer people. Because of their scarcity, those who play these instruments are in greater demand than others, and this makes playing them more "lucrative."

I remember the first time Jonathan auditioned with his flute for a place in the Southern Californian Honor Orchestra and discovered that there were eight candidates competing for every flute seat in the orchestra. His oboist friend was competing against only two candidates for a similar spot. That was when I learned that the flute was a very "competitive" instrument. Until that time, I had only considered it a very beautiful instrument. The concept that some instruments are more in demand than others had not crossed my mind. But the fact is that there are fewer oboe players than flutists, so there are simply more opportunities for oboists, whether these players are in middle school or in professional orchestras. There are more clarinetists than bassoonists. There are more violinists than violists and bassists. Furthermore, all instrumentalists are not equally valued. Professional orchestras reward their performers unequally, and the principal oboist or the principal French horn player earns considerably more than do the trombonist or flutist.

Not infrequently students switch to one of the less popular instruments simply to increase their opportunities in the music world. Indeed, teachers sometimes make that argument to students and especially to their parents when encouraging them to study French horn or euphonium (a brass instrument that looks like a small tuba). "You will have less competition," they are told. "You will find more doors open to you in the world of music."

These are sometimes called the "scholarship instruments," since parents, students, and some teachers believe that a child has a better chance of winning a college scholarship by playing one of them. One Illinois parent made the decision for his daughter—she would play the bassoon. He found a used bassoon in the school orchestra for his daughter to start on, calculating that this would maximize her scholarship potential come college-application time. I am not recommending this approach, but it is important to know that maximizing opportunity is a factor in the decisions made by some students and their parents.

- **Need-Based Instrument Selection**

Many, if not most, young musicians make their first acquaintance with orchestral instruments in a school music program. One mother in Glendora, California, said that her son chose to play the cello because his school offered either that or singing, and singing was "way uncool." A girl in St. Louis started on the violin simply because when she was in fourth grade, she won the lottery for who got to use the school violin for the year.

By far, however, the most frequently cited reason for selecting a school instrument is simply that the instrument was the one available, or a player was needed by the music teacher to fill out his orchestra or band. If the band director needs to "fill a slot," an willing student agrees to be the "filler" and may begin, in this mindless way, a lifelong commitment to an instrument. Students give this explanation over and over, especially students who play the more unusual instruments such as the euphonium or tuba. A boy from Nebraska remembered that he started playing the tuba when his band teacher needed a player. The teacher lent him a tuba, and he found that he really liked its notes and its rhythms and its mouthpiece. He felt that he was needed to fill an important place in the school orchestra. That is always a good feeling to have, especially if you are an insecure teenager looking for your place in the stratified and confusing society of the American high school.

That's how Andrea came to play the trombone. She had been taking piano lessons for years and had become proficient on the piano. In addition, she had "fooled around" on both the clarinet and the oboe. What she loved best, though, was jazz. The jazz band at her school had no place for the piano, clarinet, or the oboe, but they did need a trombone. She had never aspired to play the trombone, but when the band director asked for a trombonist, she gamely volunteered to learn how to play it. After the band director taught her "trombone fundamentals," she quickly mastered the instrument, thanks to her previous musical training. Now Andrea is "Andrea, the girl on the trombone," and she is very happy with her new role. "Playing jazz is cool," she says. The slot that she agreed to fill became her new identity.

- **Price**

If filling an available slot is a banal way of selecting an instrument, then so is picking what is cheap. That is how Darren picked the euphonium. His school band happened to have a euphonium that they

Chapter Three: You Want To Play The What?

were renting for very little money. Since this was a second instrument for him and since he was going to give it a try just to weasel his way into the band, he decided to rent it for the year. His parents could hardly object to the reasonable $30-a-year fee. Once Darren started on the euphonium, he found that he was good so he continued with it, and soon the euphonium became Darren's primary instrument. Eventually his playing outclassed the cheap school rental and he had to purchase a better quality instrument, but initially it was the minimal expense that got him started as a euphonium player.

The mother of a tuba player recalls that her son Corey actually wanted to play the saxophone.

> When Corey was in fifth grade, the band teacher invited high school students to come to the elementary school and introduce their instruments to the younger students. After the program, the fifth graders wrote their instrument choices on a parent permission card and took the card home to get a parent's signature. Corey was excited about his choice of saxophone but, as usual, he forgot the card.
>
> The next week the teacher held a meeting to introduce the instrumental music program to the parents and she also invited representatives from various music companies who stood ready to make convenient arrangements for parents to rent or purchase the instruments. At this meeting, Ms. Hooten, the teacher, gave her little talk and then got down to the nitty gritty: she needed some more students to sign up for certain less popular instruments in order to create a balanced band. Using a simple graphic, she drew a line on the chalkboard and said, "I need about this many trumpets and (drawing a second, slightly longer line below the first) I have about this many volunteers, so we're OK on our trumpets."
>
> She continued comparing her students' requests with her band's requirements, drawing parallel sets of lines on the chalkboard. When she got to the saxophone, she said, "I need this many saxophones, and this is how many kids signed up. The second saxophone line ran to the very end of the chalkboard. "And if the chalkboard were longer," she added, "the line would go on!"

I turned to Corey and told him, "Well, I guess you can forget about the saxophone. What else would you like to play?"

He blurted out, "The tuba!"

I looked at the rental information provided by the helpful companies and did not see a listing for the tuba. When Ms. Hooten asked if anyone had questions, I raised my hand. "I don't see the tuba listed here," I said. "How much would it cost to rent a tuba?"

She laughed and said, "Oh, you won't have to pay anything for a tuba rental. The school would provide you with an instrument, because the actual rental would be prohibitive."

Turning to Corey, I said, "I think that's the instrument for you."

The selection of an instrument can be made in a number of ways: it can be made with divine certainty, as a fluke, or as a cold, calculated decision. The truth is that the ways children decide on instruments has little bearing on their love for music or their future success as musicians. But this process does make for good stories to tell in later years.

CHAPTER FOUR

HELPING YOUR CHILD SELECT THE "RIGHT" INSTRUMENT

Is it really so important that children learn to play the musical instrument that is "right" for them? The answer, according to the experts, is a resounding "yes." The good news is that the process of selecting an instrument can be one of trial and error. In this process, what's important is to do what you already do as a parent: listen to your children and pay attention to what they are telling you.

As we saw in Chapter Three, children will often "lead" in selecting an instrument. A child may pick an instrument for many different reasons, and those reasons may or may not be understandable to their parents. In this chapter, we will look at what parents need to know in order to guide their child in the selection process.

Here is what music professionals report: students studying music in professional music conservatories are not more "musical" than their peers in other fields. How could this be? The reason given by researchers is that the non-musicians didn't have a chance to "become musical" because, as children, they had chosen the wrong instrument! If they had chosen the instrument that was "right" for them, they would have been likely to continue playing music.[35]

This makes instrument selection a more serious matter. With all those instruments, how do people find their way to the "right" one? With all those choices, how does anyone narrow the field to just one? And, if you choose the "wrong" one, are you stuck?

Here are some simple guidelines: a child should start on an instrument that fits his or her body and personality, and should like the way the instrument sounds and the way it looks. You can narrow the choice by considering your child's physical attributes including motor skills, ability to sing on key, degree of maturity, and ability to concentrate. If a child starts on a particularly difficult instrument and finds it problematic, there is no reason to continue with it. Change the instrument to one that the child finds more congenial. Take time with this process and enjoy it rather than letting it frustrate you. Just exploring different instruments is educational and can be lots of fun if done in a playful spirit of trial and error.

If you are a parent wanting your children to study music, you can go with them to concerts, music stores, and school orchestras to see what they find appealing. Most children have real preferences even if they're based on seemingly insignificant factors. If at all possible, their wishes should be respected. Different instruments make different physical and temperamental demands on the player, and acquainting yourself with these demands helps narrow your choices. In the rest of this chapter, we'll look at the different categories of instruments and at some of the requirements for playing them.

Chapter Four: Helping Your Child Select the "Right" Instrument

- **Playing a String Instrument**

If your child wants to play a string instrument, the common choices are the violin and the cello. One excellent reason for choosing a string instrument is that strings are manufactured in child-friendly sizes, so that even very small children can handle them—hence the phenomenon of the two-year old violinist who puts down a bottle to pick up a violin.

One reason the strings are popular is because the Suzuki program favors them and trains teachers in its method. As a result, there are many good beginning string teachers. Another reason is that there is abundant music written for solo violin and solo cello, and also for violin or cello with piano accompaniment.

Once a child studies the violin or cello, it is easy to switch to any other string instrument if he or she wishes to. Usually violinists switch to viola and cellists switch to the bass, either because they prefer the larger instrument or because this is what their school orchestra has a need for.

Playing a string instrument requires a "good ear," which means hearing when the note produced sounds "right." The note must have a good quality—clarity, tone, and control—and must be at precisely the correct pitch. This is called "intonation." Players must put the appropriate left-hand finger on the perfect spot on the string in order to produce the right note, which requires excellent fine motor control. Good gross motor control of the hands and arms, and good muscular coordination are also needed. It is not easy to make small precise movements with the left hand while simultaneously making large sweeping movements with the right. But left-handedness is neither an advantage nor disadvantage for string players. In order to play the violin and viola comfortably, however, the youngster does need to have enough strength to hold the instrument in place without tiring too easily.

String players need discipline and usually are, or soon become, self-disciplined in their habits and in their approach to the instrument.

Perhaps most important, because the instrument will certainly not give a child much immediate gratification, the beginning string player must be able to tolerate a prolonged period of frustration, and the student's family must be able to tolerate with good humor the screeching and scratching that the child initially produces. Sounding good and mastering the violin require years of study and practice.

1.   The Violin and Viola

Beginning violins come in 1/16, 1/10, 1/8, ¼, and ½, and ¾ sizes, and they have fine tuners (instead of pegs) on all the strings. Adjusting these tuners to tighten or loosen the string raises or lowers its pitch. Young children need help in tuning their instruments and their teachers (or parents) usually have to do this for them.

Violas are sized by inches rather than fractions. To determine the right-sized instrument, the child's arm is measured from the shoulder to the elbow, but many professionals who provide instruments can simply look at a child and say, "You're a 14." As the child grows, he usually trades in a smaller rental instrument for the next size up, until he is able to play on a full-size instrument. Most string shops have arrangements for accommodating children's growth and parents' pocketbooks. Besides shops, instruments can be found on-line, and at music schools. Professionals in your area will know where to find the best selections.

You *must* try out several student instruments to find the one that best suits your child. Ideally you can do this with the guidance of a professional, like a teacher. The instruments may look identical, but they will not sound identical, and the one that is easy for your child to get a good sound from may not work at all for the next student.

A Florida mother said that it took eight tries before they found the right instrument for her son, but when they did, "he could play out of tune and it still sounded great. And it was easy for him to play it."

Chapter Four: Helping Your Child Select the "Right" Instrument

The violinist and violist may have similar instruments, but they are said to have very different personalities. Violists are sometimes thought to be ex-violinists who didn't quite make the grade and decided to switch to a less competitive instrument. But the viola is the most difficult string instrument to keep in tune and to play in tune, which makes it unsuitable as a beginning instrument, although it is most suitable for jokesters. Examples abound: "How many violists does it take to change of light bulb?" "None, they can't go up that high." Or, this cruder one: "How can you get three violists to play in tune?" "Shoot two of them."

2. The Cello

The violin and the viola have a great advantage over the cello and the bass: they can be easily carried. (But the flip side of this is that they can also be more easily lost or stolen!) Most of the string instruments are carried in "hard" protective carrying cases, but hard cases are not made for the small-size cellos, which, as a result, can be damaged more easily. Because of this, parents of young cellists should be prepared to do a lot of the carrying themselves. A parent in Pennsylvania admitted that this was a problem.

> If I had known what I was getting into," she said, "I would have insisted instead on the violin! I couldn't let her carry her little cello, so I had to do it myself. Plus carrying her chair.

Cellos for young players come in 1/12, 1/10, 1/8, ¼, ½, and ¾ sizes, but there are some children and teachers who prefer to use a viola and stand it up with a pin like a cello. How you are going to transport the cello also has to be considered. If you plan to start with a cello, measure the interior of your car, remembering that your child will eventually need a full-size instrument. Some families of high-school cellists have simplified their lives by keeping one cello at home for practice and one at school for orchestra rehearsal.

The cello has several advantages over the violin and viola. Cello parts are simpler to read, holding the instrument is easier on the body, and the sound produced by a beginning cello is not as discouraging as that of a violin. Playing the cello suits some children who are "quiet" and is also popular with some children who have low voices. Sometimes children with large hands choose the cello because of how good it "feels" in their hands when they play it.

3. The String Bass

The string bass, too, is well suited for children who have large hands, especially if they have long fingers and a wide finger span. It is an excellent choice for a child who likes jazz.

When asked how best to help parents of a child new to the bass, experienced parents agreed that the key thing was to buy a big car. Most families buy a van. The parent of a bassist tells about what buying a car meant for her family:

> When the car salesman asked what we were looking for, we would go drag the bass out and try putting it into the various cars for sale. I don't think any of the salespeople had ever seen a bass, and they certainly had no feel for transporting one. Once we were told, "It's tight, but couldn't you balance it over the back of the rear seat?" Yes, I guess we could have… if we wanted to end up with a pile of kindling.

When a bassist travels by bus, the bass may have to ride down below with the luggage, which can be anxiety-producing.

Bassists generally use soft cases to protect their instruments. There are, however, hard cases for basses, which are very expensive (in the $4,000 range) and are owned by orchestras needing to transport their instruments. Individuals can rent a hard case if they need to fly with their bass. If they don't have a hard case, they will need to buy a second seat on the plane for their instrument!

When Zac had to fly from Los Angeles to New York for some college auditions, he didn't yet own a hard case, so his family made arrangements with the airline to fly the bass in a seat of its own. When they boarded the plane, they were dismayed to find that the

Chapter Four: Helping Your Child Select the "Right" Instrument

bass would not fit in a coach seat, so they had to buy two first-class seats, one for Zac and one for his bass! His mother, who accompanied him in the coach section, tells about that memorable trip east:

> When we finally got ourselves and the bass loaded on the plane, we sat at the gate for a long time wondering what was causing the delay. We were finally told that the pilot refused to fly with the bass, as he saw it as a security risk! He wanted to take the neck and scroll off the bass so that it would be shorter! Somehow he thought that would be less hazardous. Of course, Zac explained that that was impossible. The pilot ordered him and his dangerous bass off the plane! When I came on the scene, I was told not to worry, that the airline would reimburse us for our tickets. But we had to be in New York the next day for Zac's Juilliard audition! After some heated words and a lot of grumbling from the poor passengers who had been forced to sit on the plane throughout the hour-long deliberations, we and the bass were finally allowed to fly.

An alternative to buying the bass its own seat is to send the bass as luggage which, of course, means worrying about whether the "luggage" will arrive safely.

One boy, flying from a summer festival in Germany home to the West Coast, had his bass in a hard case and checked it in as required. He arrived home safely, but the bass did not. It took two days for the airline to find the bass in Kansas where it had been deposited during a brief stop. But at least it was found and was in good condition.

Another student, Ian, disembarked from his plane, looked for his bass at the baggage claim section, heard a loud thump, and saw a baggage handler picking his bass case off the floor where he had dropped it face-side down. The blow had put a fist-size hole in the face of the instrument. Upon reading the fine print on the baggage claim ticket, Ian learned that the airlines accept no responsibility for any loss or damage to musical instruments.

Not only can flying be challenging, but so can driving with string instruments. No string instrument should ever be left in a car for any length of time. In addition to the possibility of theft, there is the more usual risk of sun or heat damage to the instrument.

- **Playing a Woodwind Instrument**

The good news for parents is that woodwind instruments require a minimal amount of parental effort. For students, the good news is that no special musicality or sense of pitch is required. Even children who can't carry a tune can do very well on the flute or the clarinet, and these instruments give quick results and allow rapid achievement. The oboe and bassoon take a good deal more time to master and are usually started at a later age.

Some people worry about starting their child on a woodwind instrument, thinking woodwinds may require children to have some special physical attributes. But there is no need for enormous lung capacity, nor do wind instruments damage the heart, as is sometimes thought. It's true that beginners may feel dizzy or may pant when they first begin playing a wind instrument, but this passes quickly. Nor do a child's lips become misshapen by playing a woodwind instrument. What *is* true is that playing woodwind instruments exercises lip muscles, which increases their strength and tone. Some teenagers (namely wind players) swear that woodwind performers make superior kissers. What is fact, however, is that wind instruments can benefit certain orthodontic problems—the clarinet, for example, can help correct lower jaw protrusion. But orthodontia can interfere with playing a wind instrument, so it's best to consult with your dentist or orthodontist if you are concerned about this.

- **Which Woodwind Instrument?**

1.   The Flute

With all its levers and buttons, the long, thin flute looks like a complicated machine. But ironically, the more complicated an instrument is mechanically, the easier it is to play. (The violin is a simple machine consisting of only four taut strings, but it is incredibly difficult to play because all the work must be done by the performer.)

Chapter Four: Helping Your Child Select the "Right" Instrument

The complicated machinery of the flute actually makes it an easier instrument to master.

The flute can be played quickly with good accuracy. Unlike string instruments, the flute does not require a particularly good ear for finding the correct pitch, making it popular with beginners. Another advantage of the flute is that it can be taken apart and put together easily, and it is small and light enough to be carried about with ease. Because it is so popular, however, flutists face heavy competition for spots in an orchestra.

The flutist blows over an open hole which doesn't require a lot of strength, but it does require good lip control. Because the instrument requires blowing a lot of air, some children can get dizzy initially, but this phase doesn't last. Most children enjoy the feeling they get from all that blowing. Very thick lips, however, can present difficulties for the flutist.

The flutist uses eight fingers and the left thumb, so it is not well suited for a child who has difficulty with finger coordination. Furthermore, the flute player cannot see what those fingers are doing.

The flute is a beautiful solo instrument with an angelic sound. Both shy and sociable children enjoy the flute, but aggressive or dominant youngsters may need to make more noise and release more energy than playing the flute requires.

2. The Clarinet

Many people feel that the best single-reed instrument to start children on is the B-flat clarinet. It has many advantages. It is held comfortably in a natural arm position in front of the body and players can see their own hands. The beginner can easily get a sound out of it, so initial progress can be made quickly. The clarinet can make a big sound and its range corresponds to the lower register of a boy's voice, making it especially appealing to some boys. Because of its large range, however, reading music written for clarinet is harder than reading music for flute or oboe.

Good finger control is important for the clarinetist. Strong front teeth may give the clarinetist a slight advantage, because clarinetists use their teeth to bite down hard on the mouthpiece.

Clarinetists are able to buy ready-to-use reeds (unlike oboists and bassoonists, as we shall see.) This may be the reason clarinetists are reputed to have mellow dispositions. Clarinet reeds wear out quickly and must be changed frequently. Each player prefers a different kind of reed, so finding, adapting, or making one's own reeds can become a challenge and take a great deal of time. Beginners who buy a box of reeds can usually use all of the 10 reeds in a box. Professional clarinetists, however, buy boxes of reeds from which only two or three, when shaped and adjusted, will be adequate to their more sophisticated requirements. The rest may be used as practice reeds. If your child is handy and enjoys solitary craftsmanship, it is a good bet that shaping reeds will provide a lot of satisfaction.

Although ready-made reeds are available, buying them is chancy. It can be similar to buying a whole watermelon—you don't always get the finest quality merchandise. Clarinetists might have to buy two or three boxes of reeds to find one that they feel is satisfactory. Furthermore, as a student's playing improves, his requirements for quality reeds increases proportionately. The mother of a Kentucky high school clarinetist explains this progression:

> Before, we could go buy a box of the things for a few bucks. Now they are costing us $20 a box and even that's not good enough for Dylan any more. Now they have to be a certain brand and a certain shape. I think that real professionals may change their reeds every time they perform. We're not at that place yet! But you know how it is with shoes? When you've got a pair of shoes that cost ten dollars and then you get to the stage where you think, "Oh, my feet are probably worth a little more than that." And you think, "Maybe I should spend a little more and they'll last a little longer and my feet will feel a little better?" Well, that's the state we're at now. We

understand we need to spend a little more to get a little better quality. But I don't know where this is all going to end!

3. The Oboe

Playing the oboe requires using a small amount of air precisely, and this means very accurate muscular control of one's breath and lips. Oboists' lips should be thin and tight, capable of being folded over the teeth to trap the reed. Lip technique for oboists is extremely difficult to master, as is breath control, which requires forcing the breath through a tight opening. Some children can get headaches doing this.

Known for being a difficult instrument, the oboe was once famously described as "an ill wind that nobody blows good." A beginning oboist, like a beginning string player, must be willing to suffer through the elementary stages of learning the instrument before being able to produce pleasing sounds. In addition, the oboist will eventually have to devote large chunks of time to making his or her own reeds. The oboe is seldom selected by a young person; usually the student starts on another instrument and only later finds his way to the oboe.

The oboe (and its cousin, the English horn) are instruments that are costly both to purchase and to maintain in good working condition. Because of the costs involved and the difficulties of mastering the instrument and making the reeds, few children take up the oboe, so there are few good young oboe players. As a result of this, however, the rare good player is in great demand. The oboe might be an excellent choice for the determined, even stubborn, child who likes a challenge but doesn't like too much competition. This is an instrument that is strongly "self-selected"—the kids who like it can't always say why, but they really want to play it.

Most novices (parents and children) are in the dark about what oboe reed-making is all about. Parents who have bought their child an oboe may be dismayed to find that they must continue putting out money for reeds. This Chicago mother says,

> It's something that just doesn't stop with the oboe. I still moan when Andy asks for my credit card so he can order more cane...but then he is one happy kid when that new cane arrives and he can start working on it. This reed making takes hours upon hours, so a child really has to like doing it. Sometimes Andy's entire lesson is spent on re-making a reed, but that's something that is part of playing the oboe. I think very few people understand this—I sure didn't when he started to play, but then I didn't think he would ever become so serious about the thing!

Oboe players are faced with the task of taking cane that grows like bamboo in the wild, chopping it into smaller rods, thinning out these pieces, narrowing their shape, and then scraping them to their own specifications. Oboists feel that they must have control over these variables, which is why they do most of their own work. Even so, like clarinet reeds, some oboe reeds turn out better than others. A high-school oboist may spend five hours a week making reeds, and that is in addition to the hours spent practicing the oboe itself.

As if that is not problematic enough, there is always the possibility of injury. Andy's mother says

> I made a rule (which I *hope* is followed) that Andy does not use the reed-cutting knife after I have gone to bed. I don't want him to wake me up for a trip to the emergency room. He has cut himself a few times, minor cuts, but as a mother, I worry about that. When Andy took up the oboe, I had expected to hear music, not knives scraping.

But let's listen to the reed business from the point of view of a college oboist.

> Reed making is an inherent part, and possibly the biggest challenge, of being an oboist. We need to "make" our instrument before we can play it. When playing on a good, fresh reed, the oboe is easier for us to control and the music is much easier to make. On a bad reed, playing can be a nightmare because we have to fight with both the reed and the oboe at the same time. (And the oboe is an eternally finicky instrument.)

Chapter Four: Helping Your Child Select the "Right" Instrument

> The ideal reed minimizes the effort we dedicate to "thinking" about playing the oboe, but it does not last forever. I have had reeds that work well for one rehearsal and never sound good again, but others that lasted for over a week. One of my recent reeds lasted through three concerts, two lessons, and two auditions, plus some minimal practice time. The concerts went well, the lessons were great, and I was successful in both auditions! That kind of reed does not come to me very often.

You can hear in Andy's voice the dedication and sheer doggedness of the oboist. And you can also sense his craftsman's pride and pleasure in his work. Perhaps because of the "finicky" nature of their instrument and the large amount of solitary time needed to make their reeds, oboists have a reputation for being high-strung, nervous individualists who are oddly and wonderfully independent.

4. The Bassoon

Bassoons are also expensive instruments to buy and to repair. A good bassoon can easily cost as much as a good used car.

The bassoon is not easy to hold—let alone play—so it is not recommended for beginning music students. The instrument is large and heavy, and no scaled down bassoons are manufactured, making it an unwieldy instrument for youngsters. It is usually not begun before the age of 13 and is often played by an adolescent as a second instrument.

The bassoon player can see neither the keys nor his fingers. The fingering is complex as well, which makes digital proficiency hard to achieve. Technical considerations and instrument size often deter younger players, but the major obstacle to playing the bassoon is the constant necessity to make reeds for this double-reed instrument. Bassoonists, like oboists, should either love patient crafting and extensive detail work, or they must learn to love it, because most of them have to devote 10 to 15 hours a week tending their reeds. Like the oboist, the bassoonist has to "make" the instrument anew every few days. Bassoonists' reeds usually last longer, though, than those of their oboist colleagues.

A bassoonist needs a good ear, a long attention span, strong concentration, good coordination, and a robust work ethic. Since they are continually adjusting their reeds and puzzling over the sound their instrument is (or is not) producing, bassoonists are said to be a bit eccentric (but basically harmless). Other orchestra members joke that bassoonists work for Santa Claus, like little elves, making small wooden toys all year round. Bassoonists are said to be responsive and pleasantly gregarious with a quiet sense of humor. They can be the practical jokers of the orchestra.

- **Playing a Brass Instrument**

The bright shine and powerful sound of brass instruments appeal to most youngsters. These instruments offer many advantages. Beginning instruments are cheap, easy to care for, and long lasting. And brass lessons are less expensive since they are usually given in small groups or bands. This also makes them a popular choice for sociable kids who enjoy group lessons. A brass instrument requires a lot of energy to blow, so playing them releases pent-up energy and is good for the kid who literally needs to "blow off steam."

All brass instruments evolved from the hunting horn. With such parentage, it is not surprising that brass instruments have a sporting or military quality. The trumpets are the "jocks" of the orchestra and tend to appeal to athletic kids. Trombones are the football players, the power houses of the orchestra, and the tuba is the line blocker. French horns, more regal and sophisticated than the others, play the role of quarterbacks.

To be a successful brass player, a child needs a sensitive ear. He or she also needs lips able to produce a satisfactory sound on the mouthpiece, since only the lips (rather than reeds) do the vibrating. Most brass instruments use only three fingers of the right hand, which makes them good choices for left-handers.

Chapter Four: Helping Your Child Select the "Right" Instrument

The easiest brass instruments to start on are the trumpet and the trombone, but young players need arms strong enough to hold their instruments in a proud, upraised position—the arms of trumpeters and trombonists don't rest naturally the way oboists' and clarinetists' do.

Very young children are not likely to begin their musical education on a brass instrument, since these instruments are not made in small sizes and since playing them requires a more mature body. But a child can handle one of the brasses by the time he is 10 or 11.

Professional brass players have a reputation for being large, self-confident, and funny members of the orchestra. They have to be a certain size to hold their instruments and to have the air-power to blow them. Self-confidence is required, since even the best brass players make mistakes and, when they do, everyone hears them. Maybe their sense of humor comes from having to laugh off their bloopers.

- **Which Brass Instrument?**

1.   The Trumpet

The trumpet is a powerful, energetic, aggressive instrument—good for strong and dominant kids. Trumpeters have to strain hard to reach their high notes, making this instrument unsuitable for delicate children. Those who enjoy playing the trumpet are often independent individualists, unafraid of making mistakes.

Trumpet players start with a B-flat trumpet and may then add other trumpets to their repertoire. Since having trumpets in different keys eliminates the need to transpose (i.e. read the music in one key but play it in another), some people feel that students should stay with the B-flat trumpet until they learn to transpose mentally.

Students begin studying brass instruments at the same age they may require orthodontia, and this can be a significant problem. Braces can affect the playing of all brass instruments, but it is particularly difficult for the trumpet player. Without some protection (such as simple putty to cover the braces) young brass players can get sores and even scars on the inside of their lips that might prevent them from ever reaching a high degree of excellence. When Jerrod got braces, reports his mother,

> It was really tough. We tried different things, but none of them worked real well. The orthodontist came up with tubing that fit over the braces and kept Jerrod's lips from getting cut and swollen. The braces were a real adjustment and they've been on now for over a year. We understand that getting them *off* is also a major adjustment. When Jerrod first got them on, he lost both the high and the low notes on his trumpet. Now he's regained about 90% of what he'd lost, but he has to be careful, because if he strains too hard, he'll cut his lips up good.

For Jerrod and his family, playing the trumpet was evidently worth the struggle. Braces don't present an insurmountable obstacle, but they need to be carefully considered when your child plays the trumpet.

2. The Trombone

Playing the trombone requires a flowing movement of the right arm which makes it a good choice for kids who like to move with the music. It has a smooth energy, similar to the feeling of ice skating. For kids who like to sing, the trombone is a good choice since it is the brass instrument which comes closest to giving the feeling of singing. Its tenor register appeals to many children. Well-rounded musicians enjoy the trombone, which is a very versatile instrument, good for jazz and also for brass choirs. Yet trombone music is not too demanding and, for most children, the instrument is not too heavy.

The trombonist requires a very good ear and the same kind of sensitivity to pitch that playing a string instrument requires. This instrument can be a lot of fun for an artistic or creative child who enjoys finding and shaping each note. Since there are no valves on the instrument or markings on the trombone slide, the player must listen carefully to the sound and adjust the intonation accordingly.

Trombonists need an accurate hand to hit the precise location of that pitch-perfect spot. But this instrument does not require good finger control. Actually, it is the only instrument which doesn't require finger control. Would-be trombonists do need to have arms long enough to reach the end of the slide, which means that this instrument can be started only when children are about 11-years old.

One of the problems with the trombone is that it can be easily dented, making it less than ideal for a child who is not careful with possessions. Dents in the bell don't have to be removed, but, if there's a dent in the slide, the trombone will not function properly. Because dents don't look so lovely, most students want theirs fixed. Though professionals can remove the dents, the cost of this maintenance adds up. One exasperated mother said, "Madeleine has had so many dents that now we make her pay for fixing them herself. Our new policy is making her a lot more careful with her instrument."

3. The French Horn

The French horn is treasured for its beautiful, haunting sound. Like the trombone, it requires a player to have a good ear in order to find the correct pitch. Of all the brasses, the French horn requires the best lip control, since very small lip adjustments are necessary to determine the pitch of each note. To mute the horn, players use their fists, and this is a tricky skill to master. So is reaching the low notes on the horn.

All these requirements make the French horn a particularly difficult instrument to play well and, unfortunately, this is often obvious to concert goers. Many a student orchestra sounds reasonably good until the all-too-noticeable entrance of the French horn. For this reason, a child who wants to play the horn should have thick skin. Even the best of horn players experiences the embarrassment of hearing their instruments "crack" jarringly—usually during a quiet passage.

What makes matching pitch particularly difficult for horn players is that each note has several different fingering positions, and each fingering gives a slightly different tone and pitch. One finger position on the horn's three valves can produce up to 20 different notes! Only an excellent sense of pitch will enable the player to find the right tone using fine lip-muscle control. "Getting the correct pitch was so hard for Leah at first," says the mother of a Southern California horn player, that

> we had to use a piano to find the note for her to match. If we hadn't had a piano in the house, I don't know how she would have done it. I played the note on the piano and she tried to match the note on the horn.
>
> You really have to want to play the horn, because it's so hard to do. It is possible to play an entire scale without using any valves—just using your mouth and your hand in the bell. Because of this, finding the right pitch can be a nightmare.

Students as well as professionals have their horns cleaned every six months by a professional who can also remove the small dents that the horn has suffered.

The French horn player's breath introduces moisture, bacteria, and oil particles that mix with dust particles and settle inside of the coils of the horn. Because of this, the horn requires its own form of personal hygiene and is the only one of the instruments that has to be *bathed*. Players swab the inside of their instrument, and they also give it a warm bath (or even an acid bath) in the bathtub. After the bath, each part of the horn is towel-dried. In addition, the mouthpiece needs to be rinsed out frequently. Because of the accumulation of bacteria and dust, some parents fear that their children will be unduly exposed to diseases, but this concern appears to be unfounded.

Because it is such a challenging instrument, teachers in school orchestras often offer the horn only to the "smart kids," or to kids who take well to challenges. Heather's mother doubted that her daughter could play the horn but, she said,

> My doubts just urged Heather on. She likes to do things people don't think she can. She succeeded in spite of all the

Chapter Four: Helping Your Child Select the "Right" Instrument

warnings to the contrary and Heather has thrived on the more challenging music.

Heather is now a respected high-school hornist in Connecticut.

Horn players are justifiably proud of their nobly-shaped instruments and usually develop a close and exclusive social group. Because of all the challenges it presents, however, the French horn is clearly not a suitable beginner's instrument. However, the student who masters the horn will be very much in demand by both amateur and professional orchestras.

4. The Tuba

The tuba (along with other large brass instruments) is not the best choice for a beginner. They are harder to find, harder to maintain, and initially harder to play. Surprisingly, though, the tuba takes less physical energy to play than the trumpet or the diminutive piccolo, since its size does the work of amplifying the sound for the player.

The tuba is hard to transport and to store. Playing the tuba can be a bit lonely, since there is only one in each standard orchestra. But reading tuba music is relatively easy and the notes it plays are usually longer and more repetitive.

Professional tuba players are often large men, because it takes a lot of breath to fill a tuba, and smaller bodies just don't have what it takes. Playing the tuba is like being a hockey goalie—you often have to wait around without a lot to do, but when you are needed, your services are crucial to the team.

- **Playing a Percussion Instrument**

Classical percussionists will need to master about 30 different instruments, including several different keyboard instruments such as the xylophone and the marimba. For most percussionists, however, the tympani is king—it is both the most difficult and the most rewarding instrument in the percussion section.

Playing any percussion instrument requires good motor coordination and an extraordinarily good sense of rhythm, of course, but it is hard to judge the rhythmic capabilities of ten-year olds. Drummers are often those kids who "fidget" and discharge their nervous energy by drumming on random surfaces. Since percussionists play a large number of different instrument, kids who tend to start one thing and then leave it for something new often enjoy playing in the percussion section.

There is an erroneous belief that a percussion player does not have to have the same level of musical skills as other orchestral musicians. Real honest-to-goodness skill *is* necessary. Even playing that silly little triangle requires a special "beater," physical dexterity, and some finesse. Tuning a kettledrum while the orchestra is playing demands a high speed of execution, an exceptionally good ear, and enormous talent. It is true however that, for a raw beginner, the percussion section can often provide easy entrance to the school's orchestra program.

One of the nice things about being a percussionist in high school is that the school provides the full range of instruments. At home, the student needs only mallets, practice pads, and keyboards for practicing, so no heavy investment is required.

Percussionists are always "the ones in the back of the orchestra" and often they sit with little to do but count the bars until they get to play again. Sometimes they are made to feel less musically "worthy" than their string-playing friends. Perhaps because of this, they tend to get into trouble, especially in high school. These are the kids who play pranks or wear crazy outfits. They can be real cut-ups, the ones who make trouble for their teachers but make rehearsals fun for their classmates.

1.   The Harp

The harp is a difficult instrument to master; a performer needs good hand coordination and excellent eye-hand coordination. Unlike the

Chapter Four: Helping Your Child Select the "Right" Instrument

violin, which sounds so awful in the hands of a raw beginner, the novice harpist doesn't sound all that bad. However, it requires great skill to make the harp sound really good.

Since playing the harp involves the use of the whole body—back, arms, and legs—the harpist needs a certain amount of physical strength. Tendonitis, an inflammation of the tendons caused by repetitive use, can be a risk for some harpists but this (and similar physical problems encountered by other instrumentalists) occurs only at an advanced stage when the performer is practicing many hours a day. Good preparation for playing the harp is playing the piano.

The child who wants to play the harp should be independent and comfortable being on his or her own. Unlike other instrumentalists, the harpist will not fade into a section, but will always stand out. Because they don't belong to any subgroup of performers, some harpists say they feel a bit left out.

A major drawback to starting to play the harp is its high cost. In addition, finding an appropriate teacher is not easy, so it may be necessary to travel. However, perhaps the most serious problem with the harp (like the bass), is moving it: a harp is hard to carry, and it's hard to transport. Special adjustments may have to be made.

When Kate, a harpist in Virginia, was about to get her own instrument, her parents went around to station wagon dealerships brandishing a tape measure. "We found," her mother said,

> that her harp just fit into a Toyota Cressida station wagon—with the back seat down. Her father constructed a 4x8 board (inelegant but effective) attached to wheels and covered with foam, with a hinge that allowed Kate to fold it up. This made it possible for Kate and me to load the harp into the car. Kate could finally do it by herself only when she was a senior in high school. I lived in fear that Kate, driving by herself, would take a wrong turn one day and wind up in a terrible neighborhood with this monster of an instrument making her a wonderful target.

2.   The Piano

You may hear it said that a child with large or wide-set hands is well suited to the piano, but there is no evidence for this. Anyone can easily begin on the piano. What makes piano playing difficult is the number of notes that are played at the same time on two different staffs. A great deal of coordination and synchronization is necessary to watch your hands going in different directions and doing entirely different things. Using foot pedals adds to the motor challenges of the piano. But since the piano requires no other instrument to accompany it, it is ideally suited to the child who enjoys solitary activities, and it makes an excellent choice for a beginner.

At more advanced levels, the piano is an extremely competitive instrument. An orchestra needs a pianist only on occasion, not on a regular basis. There are many more outstanding pianists than can be employed. As professionals, pianists face enormous competition in the professional world, whether they are playing in orchestras, in chamber music ensembles, accompanying voice and other instruments, or performing as soloists. But the piano is found and played everywhere, and it is clearly the best instrument for giving a child a sense of the "big picture" of music.

*****

This chapter described the characteristics of instruments with an eye towards helping parents match their children's strengths and personalities to different instruments. It should help parents find a suitable instrumental "fit" for their child. Children who start on an instrument that suits them are far more likely to continue playing than those who are not as compatible with their instrument.

A more technical description of each instrument describing how instruments belong to "sections" and create an orchestra can be found in the Appendix, "Overview of the Orchestra."

CHAPTER FIVE

OBTAINING AN INSTRUMENT

- **Where to Search**

Where, oh where, do you find the right instrument for a beginner? For starters, try your child's school. Schools offering music programs usually have a cache of well (or poorly) used instruments. My son discovered a double bass (missing its strings and bow) in the basement of his middle school. He asked if he could rehabilitate the bass and found that the orchestra teacher was only too happy to get rid of it. Jonathan took it home, bought and attached new strings, found (in a different school building) a hairless bow, located a professional to restring it, and finally he had for himself an instrument that he played for years.

But schools also have a supply of donated and even newly purchased instruments in good repair. They are just waiting for the right student to come along and claim them. Schools usually rent these instruments on a yearly basis for a ridiculously low fee. Renting a school instrument is a tried, true, and inexpensive way to find out if your child is at all interested in playing it.

However (and this is a big "however"), as soon as it becomes clear that your child is interested in playing the instrument, it becomes absolutely necessary to find one of better quality. Playing an inferior instrument is more difficult and less satisfying. It is guaranteed to retard any child's progress and dampen his or her enthusiasm.

The best technique for finding a quality instrument, like finding anything else, is to ask around. Ask people you know and people you meet. The mother of a tuba player tells that her son's music teacher "had a daughter who had a boyfriend up in Boston who had a friend who had a tuba. So we drove up there and bought it." Like they say, "You never know." It certainly doesn't hurt to use your network and let people know what you're looking for. Especially well connected people. You could always get lucky.

Many people have electronic luck using eBay. The West Coast mother of two wind players swears by eBay. That's where her boys bought their instruments, a flute and a trumpet:

> Neal bought one flute on eBay and then decided he wanted a different one. He sold it for more than he had paid for it. With that money, he bought a nice German flute, a beautiful flute, two years old. He could hit every note right off the bat with that flute and we only paid $260.50 for it. Why the 50 cents? We out-bid the other guy by those 50 cents. My other son Jarrod snagged a trumpet on eBay that is valued at $1200 and he got it for only $375! There was a buy-it-now option with a phone number. Jarrod had already decided which make and model he wanted, and he was able to get it. We also got a lovely music stand that way. And a little light for the stand.

You can certainly explore the internet. Most people, however, still buy their instruments from shops in the neighborhood where they live or at music stores downtown. There they can see, touch, and play the instruments. Most stores that sell musical instruments have rental

Chapter Five: Obtaining an Instrument

programs and these can be beneficial. "Rent-to-buy" programs allow you to put your rental fees towards the price of purchase, should you decide later to purchase an instrument. Your school or your teacher may recommend a shop, you can scout the internet, and you can always consult the Yellow Pages. What is essential, even for a rental instrument, is that your child is allowed to try it out and play it for his or her teacher. One Florida family simply went to the local Sam Ash store where they found a little violin for $300. Their teacher thought it was an excellent buy.

- **Finding a String Instrument**

String players generally need a better quality instrument than their school can provide.

If you are buying a string instrument, there are advantages to finding a shop that specializes in strings. Most of these shops have policies that reward you for renting or buying from them. Since these children's instruments come in incremental sizes, the shops will give you full trade-in value (minus wear and tear) for the used instrument you are replacing with a bigger size. You just keep trading up. As the father of a young violist in Pennsylvania said,

> We started with a rental. When such young kids start on such tiny instruments and grow so quickly, there's no point in buying one. Colin started with a quarter size and now has a 15-inch viola, which is not quite full size, so he'll still need another one. The shop has just kept on taking back the smaller one and finding one the next size up. But expenses mount. As the violins get more expensive, so do the strings. These little violins may start at $300, but they just keep going up from there.

Music stores may not stock a supply of **string instruments** for children, but they should be willing to order a **variety** of size-appropriate instruments for you to take home, **try out, and play** for your teacher. As children grow in size, they are also **growing in** their ability to play. And as their competence improves, so **do** their demands for a better (not just bigger) instrument. Children come to **need** a more responsive instrument, one that will produce the better sound that they are now

75

capable of eliciting from the strings. This means a better made and more expensive instrument. As one parent explained,

> When you're in a certain place musically, you can't move on to a higher level until you get a better instrument. It would be wasting time and momentum to say to your kid, "Well, you just have to live with this." You have to get him what he needs so that he can grow musically. When Kevin complained of a scratchy sound on his violin, his teacher told us he needed a better violin to be able to execute harder techniques. We got him a better instrument, and when he played it, he immediately got better results. He was so thrilled with how he sounded that we knew it was worth it.

The "better" instrument is about a better sound quality. An instrument should be warm and rich and capable of projecting sound. If the *instrument* isn't able to do that, the child can never learn to do it. The better instruments have a range of sounds which train the child's ear to distinguish among them. That so-called "ear training" can't be postponed until the teen years—it must be done early in life in order for children to internalize the training.

This story, told by a mother in Kentucky, is typical of the challenges parents face in getting instruments, particularly violas, which are less popular than violins and cellos:

> The first time we went to find an instrument was difficult because they have a lot of those little *violins*, but not violas. So what we had to do is, we went to one of the stores in Louisville and they re-strung one of the little quarter-size violins that they had, and made it into a viola. They don't *make* quarter-size violas. We rented the first one because we were skeptical about whether Jim would hang in there. But he sure did. He was seven when he started, so he was already in a growing stage. It was only six months before we knew that he needed a new instrument. We rented the next one, too, but we wound up buying it.
>
> Later we heard that in Maryland they had some good violas. We called one of their 800 numbers and someone sent us several violas in the US mail for a trial period. At a place like that you don't rent, you have to buy the instruments, but

they let you keep trading them in for bigger ones until you get to a 16-incher. That's when they turn into official violas. So that's what we did. But when you get into the real violas, some of them are wider and some are thicker and what's a good fit for you depends on the size of your neck. You really have to try everything—one may have a good sound, but not be comfortable to play. So you have to look not just for the quality of the sound, but for how it fits your body. Sometimes the bows come with the instrument but now, at Jim's level, we have to buy bows separately. And we had to learn all of this the hard way.

- **Purchasing Instruments and the U.S. Mail**

When I started looking for a flute to replace the $200 Yamaha beginner's flute that Jonathan had been playing, his teacher recommended a flute seller in New York and we called him. He told us that the only way to buy a flute was to try a flute, and he offered to send us several for Jonathan to try. Which he did. I was amazed to see these valuable instruments arriving in the mail but, as I later learned, this was commonplace. The sender insures them for their value and simply assumes that the recipient of the instrument will handle them carefully, try them out for several weeks, and will return the unwanted instruments to the seller via the mail. The Kentucky mother whose son needed a viola was just as surprised as I was to learn that instruments were regularly sent through the US mail for prospective buyers to try.

While searching for a better flute, Jonathan saw a personal ad for a top-quality used flute and contacted the party in Chicago, who packed it carefully in a box and mailed it to Jonathan to try out. (This flute was valued at nine thousand dollars.) Jonathan played it for several weeks, although in the end he decided that this was not the best instrument for his needs and returned it to its owner with thanks.

- **Multiple Instruments**

Then there are the children who want more than one instrument! Most parents are amused, if nonplussed, by kids who want to own several instruments. Often these parents find they must set some kind of limit. Julie's mother is typical:

> Needless to say, after the expense of buying a clarinet and a piano, I refused to buy any more instruments, but now Julie manages to get them herself by borrowing or buying them. She bought a drum set a few years ago, took up bass clarinet last year, and this summer is playing bass guitar in a rock band.

Says this mother of a trumpeter:

> After renting a cornet, we bought it. But it didn't stop there. Jordan has gradually added trumpets as he's grown. Now we have an old decrepit B-flat trumpet that he used for marching band, another better B-flat trumpet, two E-flats, a C, a brand new E-flat trumpet, a piccolo trumpet, and a flugal horn, along with cases to hold them all.

Ah, yes, the incidentals. There are cases, and stands, and lights, and plenty of sheet music. All of these cost money, but compared to instruments and lessons, this money is small potatoes, so how can a parent say no?

Some kids want not only multiple instruments, but also obscure ones. These kids are born collectors but, instead of collecting stamps, they happen to collect musical instruments.

The mother of a horn player with this tendency says:

> My daughter likes odd instruments. She wants an alp horn, which is a long horn played standing up. They are occasionally called for in concerts but more often are played in groups at Octoberfests. She once tried a modern carbon-fiber alp horn at a French horn convention once. (Alp horns are traditional in the Swiss and German cultures.) Heather mostly wants it because it's different and "cool." Her dream list also includes a natural horn and a Wagnerian tuba. She'd really love to get her hands on a carnyx, an ancient Celtic trumpet, held vertically so the sound is ten feet above the ground. The bell is traditionally shaped like a boar's head, and the tongue and

Chapter Five: Obtaining an Instrument

> jaw move to modulate the sound. I don't believe anyone is mass producing these things.

Parents of musical children may find themselves in the music store, with barely a clue as to what it is that they are purchasing, but they have to buy the thing nonetheless. The parent of a trombonist says,

> My son's new tenor trombone had to have an F attachment. Which doesn't mean anything to me, but it meant all the world to him that his instrument had this piece on it. So we found the one he wanted and started another monthly payment.

- **Instrument Insurance**

Most beginning instruments are not valuable enough to require insurance of any kind. Once a more expensive instrument is purchased, however, insurance needs to be considered. Most instruments used by students living at home are covered by their parents' homeowner's insurance policies. However, homeowner's or renter's insurance is not all-inclusive, so that if your instrument is lost, stolen or damaged outside the house, your insurance will be of little use.

If you are looking to insure a specific or valuable instrument, there are companies specializing in the insurance of musical instruments. You can find these companies advertised in music magazines such as "Strings."

If you want to insure a $20,000 cello, for example, you can buy it for an insurance premium of about $200 a year. (Upright basses and harps, being difficult to transport, are considered high-risk instruments and have higher rates.) Some companies will insure only students or performers who play in symphonies. Many will refuse to insure rock artists or club players, citing a high risk factor.

If you are going to be flying with an instrument, know that the airlines assume no responsibility whatsoever for musical instruments. As the bass player discovered, to his dismay, airlines specifically exclude instruments from any claims filed due to loss or mishandling by airplane staff and baggage handlers.

- **The Joy of Maintenance**

Obtaining your child's first instrument may be a challenge, but there are additional challenges to come. There is the minor matter of maintenance, for example. Some instruments are easy to keep in working order; others are high-maintenance and can be expensive. Generally speaking, the more expensive an instrument is, the more costly its upkeep. Those much-in-demand professionals who specialize in repairing, cleaning, and overhauling instruments are usually very highly skilled but sometimes inconveniently located. Often players like my son learn to trust and depend on one specific person for their repairs. They will send their instrument cross country to ensure that it is worked on only by the best possible person. To be sure, this can be a hair-raising experience.

When my son's beginner's flute needed repair, we would take it to a local man who did an excellent job on it, but there was a problem: Jonathan couldn't be without his flute for the days (and sometimes a week) that it took for the repair work to be completed. He was also worried about what would happen if the flute "broke" right before a performance. One day in a flute magazine (yes, each instrument has a periodical of its own) he saw an ad: "Learn the art of fixing and overhauling flutes in my home." Jonathan's eyes widened, he called the number given, and found a man living in upstate Vermont offering a one-week, live-in class for flute specialists. He begged me for permission to attend. Since Jonathan was 14, I was not enthusiastic about the idea, but he convinced me that learning to fix his own instrument was essential. I resisted, hesitated, and finally I relented. Jonathan flew to New York City where he met this technical flute whiz, accepted his offer of a lift to his house in Vermont, lived with the man's wife and children plus one other student (a professional flute-fixer) for that week, and returned home with a new set of tools and the ability to fix his own instrument in any emergency. I am not recommending this approach! I am simply recounting this episode as an indication of how important it is for musicians to be certain that they can get their instrument worked on promptly and skillfully.

Chapter Five: Obtaining an Instrument

None of my experiences with instrument purchase or repair would keep me from giving my child a fine music education. The benefits of learning to play an instrument (see Chapters Eleven and Twelve) are vastly greater than the aggravations involved in getting and caring for an instrument. But it is useful to know that obtaining the instrument and keeping it in working order can be a quirky and fascinating experience. As the parent of a young musician, you will have experiences with your child's instruments that will introduce you to new ways of looking at things. At the very least, they can augment and stretch your sense of humor.

CHAPTER SIX

LIFE AT SCHOOL

- **Social Life**

Contrary to the stereotype of the inwardly focused, anti-social artist, the great majority of student instrumentalists carry on an active social life. "My kid doesn't fit the profile of what people expect musical kids to be," protested the father of a clarinetist. "She isn't a lonely wall flower—she is a real social butterfly." Most of these kids are interested in gymnastics, theater, athletics, the opposite sex—the regular run of teen-age activities— and they make friends both inside and outside of their musical circle of friends.

Nevertheless, quite a few of these kids, especially in their elementary-school years, don't "click" with their classmates. As one mother said, "When all the cool girls were going to soccer practice together, Audrey was going to her flute lesson and chamber music group. She was consciously different and did not run with the pack." Some kids, trying to break into a group, are self-conscious and defensive. A ninth-grade harpist wailed, "I'm only a kid. Just because I play the harp and not a lot of people do...that doesn't make me a freak, does it?"

Some young musicians are so busy with their music and other activities that their "busyness" puts off possible friends. Maricella's mother says, "My daughter is under a lot of pressure with all that she does. None of her friends are so busy. I don't think they can relate to the pressure she is under with practicing and performance deadlines." The mother of a trumpet player explained how her son's music impacted his love life:

> Miguel had a girlfriend for three years in high school, but she knew where she stood. Miguel would practice first and then go out with her. Last year, they went to the prom together, but Miguel insisted on being home by midnight because he had an audition the next morning. That meant she didn't get to go to the late night post-prom party, and she was livid.

- **Music as a Social Experience**

Music groups, especially bands and orchestras, create a social niche that can be transformative for young instrumentalists. A father whose son previously had few real friendships, saw him connect enthusiastically to other players in his orchestra and said,

> I wish *I* had his social life. These kids he has found in band... they are simply fabulous kids. White, black, Hispanic, girls, guys, they all play together in the band and after rehearsals in each others' homes. Finally, he has friends—real friends.

Especially in the middle-school and high-school years, students need validation—like all of us, they need to feel valued and valuable. They need to fit in somewhere and, for music students, the orchestra is that place. Just as athletes have their teams, thespians their stage, and techies their computer labs, musicians need their orchestras. They need a social circle, a place to make and cement friendships, a place to "hang out."

Chapter Six: Life at School

When these youngsters meet peers who share their interests, their involvement and talent in music makes them more, not less, attractive (especially to the opposite sex). Their social life becomes much more stable. One father said that his son had friends from different bands who called themselves "the band nerds," but that once his son had band friends, he no longer felt like a nerd.

I hadn't realized that my son had been feeling like a social misfit until he found himself in his first orchestra at a summer music camp. One day he told me, "I love it here. I like everybody and everybody likes me." It was only then that I realized how unhappy Jonathan had been in school. Until then, he really had not "liked everybody" because the boys in sixth grade who were into skateboarding and hockey were not like him. In the orchestra environment, however, he fit in just fine. I had never heard him tell a joke before he joined the summer camp orchestra. Suddenly he had a slew of daring ones. Example: "What's the difference between a bull and an orchestra? Answer: The bull has horns in the front and an ass in the back. The orchestra has horns in the back and an ass in the front." (Well, it was daring for a sixth grader.) In his orchestra, Jonathan had found the social life that had previously eluded him. He fit in joyfully, was respected for what he could do, and finally he was a "somebody."

School orchestras are cross-grade programs: as kids enter, they get to meet older and more experienced players who play big brother and sister to the newcomers. Colin, a Pittsburgh violist, was only 11 years old when he first joined an orchestra. As the newest (and cutest) violist, he was petted and tended by the older players in the viola section. They made sure he knew where to go, what to bring, and when to bring it. His mother said, "That was the only place where I didn't have to worry about him. The orchestra and Colin were a perfect fit and he was in violist heaven."

- **Playing in an Orchestra Improves a Child's Performance**

Playing in a school orchestra not only makes students feel good. It can also significantly improve their level of performance, both in music and in academics. Students with band and orchestra experience attend college at a rate twice the national average![36]

If students are in an orchestra, there is an important reason to practice: no students want to look foolish in front of their peers. And if there is a concert coming up next week, they want to *sound* good too because in an orchestra, it is not just one student and his instrument—all players have to think about how their instruments and their parts fit into the whole. As student musicians understand this larger framework, they become more sophisticated performers.

Parents of students in a Missouri high school, frustrated that there was no school orchestra, managed to put one together and hired a local university music professor to conduct it. They reported that their children made enormous improvements in their playing. These parents only wished they hadn't waited so long to take matters into their own hands.

- **The Role of Instrumental Music in Middle School**

When my son was in middle school (and performing with an outside community orchestra), there were basketball courts for the athletes, but no venue existed in the school for a 7th-grade flutist performing Mozart concertos. Few, if any, adults at his school knew about his extra-curricular "hobby." After hearing that Jonathan would be absent because of an upcoming solo performance, his social studies teacher posted a small article in the school newspaper entitled, "Does Anyone Know about the Virtuoso in Our School?" A good question. Jonathan was not the shy, retiring sort. The reason no one knew is that there was no occasion in the school for hearing solo instrumental music. Such performance was not included in the usual middle school activities. It's not that the teachers were uninterested. (It so happens that this social studies teacher collected three other teachers who drove to Pasadena to hear Jonathan perform the concerto with his youth orchestra.) It's that there is often no mechanism in schools for the development and encouragement of a child who is working outside of school towards an advanced level of musical accomplishment. If a talented basketball player is enrolled in a public-school 7th grade class, the school administrators know about it. But few on a school administrative staff would know about a similarly talented young musician.

However, advocates for music education have begun to do something about this situation. They are collecting statistics that tout the value of studying music, and this new information is slowly making its way into the consciousness of our educational policymakers. We know, for example, that "students who report consistent high levels of involvement in instrumental music over the middle and high school years show significantly higher levels of mathematics proficiency."[37] When it comes to our children's educations, we in the United States are a no-frills society. Despite correlations between music-making and educational success, music in many school districts in the United States is still seen as an "extra."

- **Conflicts with Sports and Extra-Curricular Activities**

Team sports practices, extra-curricular activities, and music rehearsals vie for the time, energy, and allegiance of high-school students. With homework loads increasing over the last few years, students who are trying to meet all of their commitments can become easily exhausted.

They learn, sooner or later, that they cannot do everything. Having won the Illinois State Chess championship in fourth grade, Omri, a high-school student, was saddened to give up chess when his chess match schedule conflicted with orchestra rehearsals. But even when he limited himself to music, there were scheduling conflicts. Omri played in his school's band and also in the community orchestra. What to do when each of them scheduled a rehearsal on the same night? Omri's mother, a patient person, reports:

> We would usually talk to the band director beforehand and try to work it out. Sometimes it meant leaving orchestra early to make a part of band practice—a lot of driving around for me and guilt and tension for Omri.

Here's an example of the kind of craziness such conflicts in scheduling can cause and the kinds of demanding compromises that may be required. Kass's mother recounts:

> Kass played in her school orchestra and also in the community-wide Utah Youth Symphony. One week she had Youth Symphony rehearsal almost every night in Salt Lake City. But she was in mid-basketball season and was also required to be at every basketball practice and game. On this particular night, she had a game at the high school, a Utah Youth Symphony concert, and a school orchestra performance at the local university. She explained to her school orchestra director that she was unable to attend the performance and he was quite upset. He desperately needed her. He offered to make the 30-minute drive to Salt Lake City to pick her up from Youth Orchestra and drive her back so that she could play in his ten-minute performance. He called me to see if I could help to make it happen. But the basketball coach and Utah Youth Symphony Director also needed Kass. So we called the Symphony director and Kass' coach, explaining the situation. They agreed to allow her to miss, because they realized this was just too much stress for a young woman.

Over-achievers like Kass can be stretched to their limits. So can their families.

- **Music and Athletics**

Conflicts between sports and music occur frequently in high school and can be serious issues for students. Some students who hope to be professional musicians become so concerned about the possibility of injury that they give up athletics altogether. Cellists cannot risk breaking an arm on the football field. If a flutist breaks a finger during volleyball practice, she is "toast."

But the more common problem occurs when athletic coaches require their players to be at every practice and game, conductors require them to be at every rehearsal and performance, and these obligations conflict. In these situations, frustrations can mount, tempers may flare, and tears can flow.

Chapter Six: Life at School

The father of a jazz trumpet player explained:

> Chris was a starter on his basketball team which came in third place in the Ohio State championship games. He loved to get out on that court and show his stuff. But in high school his trumpet teacher insisted that he come to all of the jazz band rehearsals and the basketball coach insisted he be at all team practices. He couldn't be at two places at the same time and so he had to say no to basketball. He was in tears when he made that decision.

Although fortunately this is not common, athletic coaches and administrators can sometimes force students to make painful, all-or-nothing choices, even when practice times for different activities only rarely conflict. A Houston mother protested:

> Ricardo's teachers didn't allow the kids to experience a lot of different things. They wanted him to commit and pick only one thing and do that one thing all the time. These teachers pigeonhole kids and make it tough on them. Ricardo's baseball coach made him sit out because he missed one practice. The coach told him, "You either are going go play on a sports team or not. If you want to play on a team, your whole life has to become that." And why? Why should it?

Kristina's mother concurs:

> My daughter loved soccer and her violin, but her soccer coach didn't let her play very much.
>
> If you're going to be on a team, the coaches want you to be there without fail. If you miss practice, especially if it's for another activity like band or orchestra, the coach keeps you benched. The administration sure didn't do much about it. They called it "policy." What kind of policy is that?

Sports are a perfect physical and social outlet for the kids who spend hours in solitary practice rooms with their instruments. The athletics department, however, is often geared to winning games, rather than educating young people. We are talking about high school, where athletics could be more about participation, exercise, sportsmanship and teamwork. Then all students—even the ones committed to music—could participate.

An Arizona clarinetist's mother pointed out that her son's regular swimming was excellent training for playing clarinet—it helped develop his breathing. Swimming (along with water polo) was my son's high school sport, too. He was dropped from the team because of a conflict with his music. Because he wanted to continue swimming in some capacity, Jonathan petitioned to be allowed to continue working out with the team. He argued his case, explaining that he wouldn't take any time away from team functions, that he just wanted to swim laps, that he loved to swim, and that it was beneficial for his flute playing. But to no avail. No exceptions were made, nor did the school administration intervene. I wondered at the time about what it might be like for a music-loving, state-ranked *swimmer*. What if he or she was on the way to a berth on the Olympic team and was making a name for the school as well as for himself? Would this swimmer be allowed to participate in a school *music* group that he or she loved, even if it wasn't possible to make all the performances? I imagine that, for a talented athlete, exceptions might be allowed because high school athletes are currently given that kind of respect.

Athletics and music can be complementary, not adversarial experiences, as this mother of an Oregon violinist eloquently explains:

> When Lee has a bad day on the basketball court, she comes home and grabs her violin. When she's practicing and can't work out a passage on the violin, she takes a break and goes outside to shoot hoops. I've seen her come home miserable about the way she played ball in the afternoon, go out that night to hear a concert, and come home with her head held high again. I think that when she doubts herself in one area but can turn around and find herself in another, it's very reassuring. It is a reminder that we are made up of many parts and that the losses we experience in one area of our life can be offset by succeeding in another. It is a reminder that the loss, or whatever, is just one small part of the big picture that is you.

It is unfortunate that our children are forced to choose between worthwhile activities. With greater flexibility on the part of teachers and coaches, well-rounded kids who enjoy different aspects of life would not need to choose among them or to take *all* of them so seriously. High school could then be a time for experimenting with and experiencing a whole host of interests and activities.

- **How School Music Teachers Influence Students**

Where a school orchestra exists, adult teachers and conductors can have enormous influence on students. Teaching music means that teachers spend intensive time with individuals. This is true of all good teachers, of course, but teaching instrumental music demands individualized one-on-one teaching. The instruction a biology teacher gives to student A can usually be given as well to student B. But what an orchestra conductor teaches the trombonist is different from what he or she teaches the violinist. When Mary Ann decided that she wanted to play the horn, her band teacher taught her the basic scales that she would need, meeting her in the orchestra room before school every morning. When Sammy felt down about his trumpet playing, his teacher took him out for a coke and some confidence-building (contemporary tea and sympathy). When Jennifer thought she wasn't up to the challenge of playing the oboe, her teacher said, "You can do it, you can do it, you can!" Jennifer got the message and found that, indeed, she could.

The film *Mr. Holland's Opus* comes to mind, Mr. Holland became an inspiration to his students and he came to see his life's work as teaching rather than composing music. His influence on his students was his great "opus." *Mr. Holland's Opus* was fiction, but the documentary film, *Music of the Heart,* is the true story of how one teacher with a violin changed the lives of hundreds of children in Harlem.

Parents recognize the debt they owe to band and orchestra teachers. The mother of a clarinetist explained that her son had been singing and playing the piano for some time, but it was the band teacher who made him into a musician. "Something musical had obviously been brewing for some time with Dylan," his mother said, "Something must have been cooking. But when Dylan got into middle school, this man (his orchestra teacher) made the mix into soup."

Music teachers are often role models for students, especially for minority students. A large study of high school students showed that African-Americans found role models in their music teachers far more frequently than they found role models in any other of their high-school teachers. In fact, a whopping 36% identified music teachers as their role models compared to only 7% who named as models their physical education teachers and coaches.[38]

It is true, however, that some school music teachers may need more training to work well with students who are also being privately taught. The level of teaching is generally strong among teachers of choir and chorus. The task for conductors of high school bands and orchestras is perhaps more difficult. To be a successful conductor of any orchestra means having a working knowledge of all the instruments, and this knowledge is even more important when working with an orchestra composed of beginning students.

The mother of a Wisconsin violinist fretted over her daughter's difficulties with the school orchestra conductor:

> He was a self-important director who was not a string player and he had little knowledge of how strings differ from wind instruments. He continually contradicted what Han's private teacher was teaching her to do. What misery that man caused!

A mother in Ohio said:

> Joseph had been happily playing the trumpet for years and was totally devoted to his instrument. But his band director actually pressed him to change to the clarinet, saying he needed to be "challenged." He needed a challenging teacher, not a change of instruments! I had to explain to the teacher that this would mess up Joseph's embouchure and this teacher had no idea what I was talking about! He just didn't know much about music. I don't know how he got to be a music

teacher. Joseph knew more about music than he did. I couldn't believe that a teacher could know less than my son did but...it was true."

More knowledgeable school conductors would contribute to improving the training available in performing arts education as, of course, would knowledgeable teachers in any field.

- **Teachers as Advocates for Students**

The best school music teachers both encourage and tutor students. They also identify talent and convince parents to do something about it. Jarrod's mother had a hard time fending off her son's persistent music teacher.

> When Jarrod said he wanted to play the trumpet, I said, "Whaaaaaat?" I thought it was another one of those things that he would do and then leave for a more exciting newest thing. But then I started getting calls from my son's music teacher at school saying, "You need to give your child private lessons." You know, we have a busy life here, and the expense of lessons...But the teacher just kept calling back. She said, "You really don't understand. You really have to get your kid lessons. He's really good and he really needs lessons." She called like five times. She would call during school and put Jarrod on the phone to me and he would say, "Mom, Mrs. Ross says I need private lessons." And, ya, ya, ya, I was completely not buying it. You know what we've got in this house? Roller blades, roller skates, skate boards, helmets. My kids had one passion after another.

Today, however, after years of private lessons under his belt, Jarrod loves his trumpet and plays it beautifully. His mother is very grateful to the teacher who made it all happen.

When Corey was in the sixth grade playing the tuba in his school orchestra, his middle school teacher, like Jarrod's, started to badger his mother about providing him with proper private lessons.

> The music teacher said she didn't want Corey to develop bad habits early in his music career. I was unconvinced. Private lessons take time and cost money. Only after I received

> another call from Corey's principal did I relent. The music teacher had enlisted her support to make sure I got Corey into private lessons. The principal convinced me to look at the lessons as an investment for college. If his talent was well nurtured, he could get a tuba scholarship to just about any university in the country, she said. And, believe it or not, this is what happened.

Corey's mother raves about the support she and her son received from this music teacher.

> Ms. Hooten, bless her heart, has continued over the last six years to maintain an interest in Corey's development. Years after he was no longer her student, she was still working to convince me to develop his potential with more and more challenging activities.

Not taking the music teacher's advice to give her son private lessons proved costly for the mother of Dylan, the clarinetist (although, of course, she did avoid for a time the cost of the lessons). When Dylan's band director suggested private lessons, says his mother,

> I was hesitating because I had been giving Dylan piano lessons and I had a lot invested in the piano. The band director kept at me, telling me to give him clarinet lessons. I never did give in to his pressure. But three years later, when Dylan auditioned for a more advanced city-wide youth orchestra and made it, he discovered that there was a prerequisite: you had to be taking private lessons to play there. So that was when I finally got him his first private clarinet lesson. When he was 14. I later found out that that was very unusual. But how was I to know? Sometimes now he wags his finger at me and reminds me that he is playing catch-up with the big dogs now. He feels like he's come to the party a little late and it's all my fault.

- **Youth Orchestras and All-State Bands**

Youth orchestras like the one Dylan found are generally city-wide or area-wide organizations that are formed by invitation only. They may have various names—youth orchestras, all-school orchestras, honor bands, or all-state bands. Outside of school, youth orchestras and bands serve young instrumentalists of the community, city, or state, and showcase the most talented among them. New York, Chicago, San Francisco and some other large cities have fine youth orchestras.

One 12-year-old violinist who had played concertos with two professional orchestras before, said his greatest thrill was not playing with the pros, but playing with a youth orchestra with kids just like him.

Students who come to audition for a youth orchestra or band perform in front of judges, and only the most accomplished candidates are accepted from the applicant pool. The players are then ranked in order of excellence and seated in "chairs," with the prestigious "first chair" reserved for the best player. The community-wide youth orchestra can be a salvation for the high school student in a school lacking one, or in a school whose orchestra performs at a beginners' level. (School districts where music education is not promoted will understandably have less accomplished school orchestras.)

Community youth orchestras can provide a sense of validation and an outlet for kids in a school or a school system where music is undervalued. Too many students say that their regular school teachers know little about their musical life. And when they do, they treat it with indifference. Some students who are serious musicians have received so little attention and encouragement from their schools that they lose interest in school itself.

Seth's mother said, "In my son's school, if they need someone to play in an assembly, they think of Seth. Otherwise, they ignore him. That's how much they value music." Or, as the mother of a trumpet player said, "Most of the teachers in our school district have no clue about good music."

A child who has had quality private music training can experience dissatisfaction in his school orchestra. This is what Jarrod's mother found:

> In his first school orchestra Jarrod got very frustrated with the music. The other kids just weren't at his level. He was the only one you could hear carrying any melody at all. He just couldn't stand it. Some of the kids don't practice at all outside of that one hour a week in school, so you don't get much musicality there. That's the problem: once you're introduced to a higher level of musicianship, you don't want to go back to the low level stuff.

Since weak school orchestras provide little challenge for gifted young musicians, you would think that schools would encourage their talented students to seek out city-wide music programs, but often that does not happen. Ironically, the schools make every effort to retain the little talent they may have but have not nurtured. An agreement is extracted from community youth orchestras: No student may play in the outside orchestra unless that student also plays with his or her own school orchestra. Here's what happened to Kelly, a Southern California oboe player:

> Kelly's school band did not perform at a very high level, so she convinced her high school band teacher to allow her to try out for the California All-State Band and she was thrilled when she got in. She told her school band teacher about her success and said that she wanted to drop out of his school band, but he said she couldn't. She had to be in the school band to play with the All-State. My kid, who is usually not this assertive, absolutely refused to go back to her school's band program. She actually found a better school band in another school and she enrolled in that school's band! I had to drive her every day back and forth between her "academic" school and her "school band" school. It was a nightmare, an absolute nightmare.

Here's how an Arizona mother dealt with her school's rule that any student who wanted to play in the concert band must also play in the marching band. The level of music in the marching band was so far beneath that of the concert band that Michael didn't want to play in it. His mother found a concert band in the community college in Scottsdale and took Michael to play there. He was only 15 years old, playing with a lot of retirees and certainly not meeting his social needs, but at least he wasn't bored.

Chapter Six: Life at School

You may say that there is a good reason for school regulations of this kind, and you would be right. It is valuable for beginning high-school music students to encounter strong performance skills in peers. But must the advanced student sit through hours of rehearsals for the sake of the others? No one would think to insist that high-school Olympic swimmers practice beginning breathing exercises for the sake of the novices. But advanced flute players regularly sit alongside and are made to practice elementary breathing exercises with flutists still struggling to learn basic scales.

My son, like other serious high school music students, was required to play in his high school orchestra to qualify for a spot in the city youth orchestra. He finally figured out a way to make it work for him. He figured the school rule was to play in the orchestra, but the rule didn't specify what *instrument* he had to play. He decided to teach himself a new instrument. In his community youth orchestra he may have been the respected principal flutist, but for his high school orchestra, he became one of the bassists. His skill level on the bass was rudimentary, so playing it in school was challenging enough to keep him interested.

- **Money and Musical Malaise**

School music programs are dying. Not everywhere, but in enough places that it is going to have a profound effect on the future of American music. We are already seeing the effects of our mediocre music system reflected in our finest professional orchestras which hire well-trained, foreign-born musicians to fill their chairs. The best young musicians in America, especially in metropolitan areas, are often the children of immigrants. In some youth orchestras whole sections, especially string sections, are filled with talented and dedicated first-generation Asian students.

We know one reason why: it's money. There is never enough of it for the public schools, and when schools have to make cuts, the first things to go are the "non-essentials." Music is a non-essential, because it doesn't prepare students for the workplace nor does it help to make them wealthy. So our music programs (along with art programs) are unceremoniously scaled back or eliminated. The general public sees music as a pleasant diversion, but unimportant. (Athletics are seen as pleasant *and* important. As a Denver area mother said, "Our school district is all for sports and has nothing for music.")

We know that colleges and universities are beholden to their sports programs for bringing in money. They lure outstanding high school athletes to come play on their teams, and the success of their sports teams is said to motivate big-donor alumni. This explains, at least, why colleges court their athletes. But the financing of high schools does not depend on alumni donations for endowed chairs. Middle schools and high schools are not in thrall to their sports programs for survival. They can and should devote as much money to arts as to athletics.

The future of music in the public schools is nevertheless uncertain—far too few schools have adequate music programs. Though there has been a great deal of media attention paid to the benefits of arts in education, and although parents by and large support music programs in the schools, most school systems have yet to respond with well-funded and well-functioning art and music departments. Of course we as parents and citizens must lobby our school boards to commit more resources to school arts programs. But until that time comes, we must be prepared to augment whatever music our children learn at school with our own resources.

CHAPTER SEVEN

PRACTICE MAKES PERFECT

One cannot decide as an adult to enter the field of music performance. Indeed, not even in late adolescence. There are virtually no professional musicians who started playing their instrument after the age of 18. A performing musician's training absolutely *must* begin in childhood. Because of this, music performance is unlike crafts such as carpentry and metalworking, or professions like law, medicine or engineering, or academic fields such as literature and the social sciences.

Training a classical musician is akin to training a ballerina or a gymnast—the required musculature and a sensitive ear must be developed from a very early age. Therefore, a child who quits (even for a year) will rarely be able to reconsider the decision when he or she is more mature. For a talented young musician, quitting is an irreversible decision. So practicing is a serious issue.

Yes, practicing is boring. Yes, it is a sore issue, not only for parents today—practice has been a challenge for parents in every generation. It is an issue, not only for parents of children with average ability, but also for parents of the most talented musicians.

Here is a story that reads like a joke, although I am told it is the honest truth. The story is not hard to believe. A San Diego father, who was concerned about his 10-year-old son's resistance to practicing his violin, discovered that Yehudi Menuhin was in town for a performance that weekend. The great violinist was staying at the home of one of the father's friends. As a way of stimulating his son's interest, this father seized the opportunity to introduce his son to Menuhin. As they entered the friend's house, they heard the sounds of a violin coming from the back room. "Is that Menuhin playing? asked the father hopefully.

"Yes," his friend replied. "He's been practicing the last two hours for his concert tonight."

The son's jaw dropped. "If Menuhin still has to practice that much," he said, "I'm quitting now."

Performing music requires practice. This is a universal truth. But problems with practicing are almost as universal. Many parents think their children's resistance to practicing means their child doesn't like music enough, and therefore that music lessons are a waste of time and money. Others feel that, if they have to police the child's practicing, music lessons are not worth the effort. Neither of these statements is true.

Most parents complain that their children don't practice enough, or that they have to *make* their children practice.

- **Jonathan's Practicing Meltdown**

When my son Jonathan got his first flute at the age of seven, he was so excited about it that he took it to bed that night. Practicing was not an issue in those early halcyon days. The weekly assignments

Chapter Seven: Practice Makes Perfect

that his teacher wrote down for him in a little spiral notebook were clearly spelled out: one scale, one piece, and one exercise. He practiced in five minute sessions, several times a day, was always prepared for his weekly lessons, and his teacher was pleased with his progress. My only tasks were to buy him basic supplies and get him to his lessons.

But as Jonathan grew and progressed musically, the teacher's requirements became more demanding and he began to slack off. He could get by with practicing less and so, being human, he did. What really motivated him during those years were his teacher's frequent recitals. She didn't cut corners on them. She hired a fine professional accompanist for the occasions, printed up bright orange programs, and provided heaps of jelly beans. The recitals motivated my child to practice, at least for the week before the recital. And that's pretty much how things continued—until around the time Jonathon entered middle school.

By the time he was 12 Jonathan hated practicing his flute with a passion. I reminded him and reminded again. Then I threatened. I shouted and he shouted back. He agreed to practice and then would procrastinate until it was too late. The flute can be piercingly loud, especially in the still of the night. We had neighbors who were neighborly and understanding—but there are limits and, in our house, the limit was 10:00 pm. At one point my temper was so frayed, I sputtered, "That's it! If you don't practice, I'm not giving you flute lessons!!" I thought the threat would work. But instead he called my bluff.

"OK, then, I'll quit!"

My tactic had backfired. Unable to retreat gracefully, I remember shouting at him, "OK, then quit! Call your teacher and tell her you are quitting!"

"*You* call her!" he said.

"No, *you*!" I screamed. "You want to quit, so *you* call her!" We went on this way for some time, both of us out of our skulls with anger. It should have been a showdown. But neither of us would actually pick up the phone to make that call. And so we backed down from our game of brinkmanship.

After that ugly climax, the worst of the problems faded a bit, but practicing continued to be difficult. By degrees Jonathon learned to discipline himself into doing it. Little by little, he began to take on himself the responsibility for practicing, but he did this only because he *did* want to play and to perform. He just didn't want to practice.

Late in high school, Jonathan became serious about his music. When he was preparing for a solo part or an audition, he would sometimes practice five hours a day and I became concerned that the boy was practicing too much!

- **Professionals' Problems With Practicing**

Some parents think if their children don't want to practice, they must not be interested in music. This is why parents give up on music lessons when their children resist practicing. I had this opinion, too, before I lived through the experience of raising a child who loved music but hated to practice. Then I read the biographies of some famous musicians, and was astonished to find that many of them exhibited similar behavior: they, too, had hated to practice!

Vladimir Horowitz, perhaps the most acclaimed pianist of the 20th century, refused to practice as a child. Horowitz' mother was exasperated and increasingly worried. From her perspective, "Here was her promising son, exceptionally gifted, who refused to practice scales and subject himself to the traditions and expected discipline. What would become of him?" [39] What became of him, as we know now, was astonishing virtuosity. We don't know exactly how it happened, but evidently Mr. Horowitz outgrew his resistance to practicing.

Chapter Seven: Practice Makes Perfect

And then there is the French composer, Ravel. Ravel's biographer describes Ravel as a lackluster child who hated to work and especially hated to practice. The biographer writes, "Ravel was not a particularly diligent pupil…he was more interested in play than in work. Various persuasions, cajolings, and admonitions were required to make him attend to his lessons and his practice…there was no hint of the infant prodigy ready to conquer the musical world in short pants and velvet suits." [40] Despite the mythical stories we hear of precocious children and their musical achievement, not all genius is apparent in childhood.

Marilyn Horne, the great American soprano, said, "As a kid, I sometimes wanted to play, go to the movies, parties, baseball games, *anything* rather than practice." [41] She sounds just like any other healthy, normal child. But practice she did, and we have her brilliant performances to prove it. She looked back on her youthful years with nostalgia, understanding, and compassion for how she behaved as a child.

Isaac Stern, the American violinist credited with saving Carnegie Hall, spent years teaching, coaching, and encouraging young violinists all over the world. As a respected pedagogue, he vividly described the tedium of practicing:

> About the matter of practice, no youngster could possibly feel enthusiastic over the drudgery that was the foundation of accomplishment. Only later, when the student became aware of an ability to create musical sounds on his own and began to experience the excited discovery that he was able to create something special, only then would he gain more interest in the work required of him. The child should practice to the extent considered minimally necessary by his teacher, but not beyond the limits of concentration.

Basing his philosophy on his own childhood experiences of "drudgery," Stern advocated that teachers place limits on their demands of students. In his autobiography, he writes that he was often unfocused and unwilling to practice. It was his mother who, he said, kept me to the practicing grind when my tendency was to be elsewhere. One day when I was ten years old, I suddenly discovered that I could do things on my own with the violin, things no one had taught me—move the bow in certain new ways; feel my fingers on the strings; bring forth shades of sound. I do not believe in moments that come out of nowhere. As I see it, what happens is an accumulation of experiences that blossom into a sudden sense of self and the ability to actually do something on one's own. These moments differ from child to child; they depend so much on what the child has been exposed to. In my case, suddenly one day I became my own master, I wanted to play; I wanted to learn how to play better. I wanted to do it because I was beginning to revel in my own abilities. That was when things changed for me; when I began to discover what I could already do and to sense the possibilities of how much more I might be able to do. Never again did I need to be urged to practice.[42]

When we hear what these brilliant professionals reveal about their childhood struggles, it puts into perspective the negativity and resistance of our own children. If your child does not want to practice, this does not mean he or she doesn't like music. It doesn't mean that he won't be successful in music. It means this child is a very typical student who is in excellent musical company.

- **Variations in the Amount of Practicing**

The amount of time that young people practice varies enormously. One factor, of course, is the child's personal make up. Some parents, like the frustrated mother of a violist in Los Angeles' American Youth Symphony, complain that their children get away with little practicing. "I shudder to think," she said, "what Jessica could be doing now, if she had spent serious time practicing as a young child." The mother of a Louisville bassist acknowledged that she was frustrated "because I saw how much talent my daughter had and how good she could be if she practiced. But then I had to step back and say, 'Wait a minute. That's my selfishness talking. I'm not her.' I had to learn to accept her limitations."

Another factor in practice time depends on the demands made by the instrument your child has chosen to play. Pianists and string players practice many more hours than do wind players. The reason is not strength of character but body mechanics. Pianists and string players can put in five hours of practicing a day without undue strain on their bodies. (We are speaking here of super-serious students at music conservatories who are pursuing careers in music and are pushing their maximum physical limits.)

The lips and lungs of the wind players cannot sustain overuse and, as a result, wind players cannot practice as many hours. Horn players can get dizzy from too much practicing. Flute players can get cricks in their necks. Oboists can break a blood vessel. But school children are highly unlikely to be afflicted with such physical problems.

For some musicians, putting in their practice time is a point of honor. At the other end of the spectrum are those who like to pretend that they *never* practiced. Glen Gould said, "I never bothered to practice very much—I now practice almost not at all—but even in those [early] days I was far from being a slave of the instrument." [43] This is a form of professional machismo, not unlike the A+ student who turns in his term paper while claiming, "I just started it last night and had to pull an all-nighter. I hope I pass."

- **Self-Motivated Kids**

Although most students at some time in their lives resist practicing, there is a sizable minority who are wholly self-disciplined. These children rarely, if ever, need reminders to practice. The fact that such children exist leads some parents to think that their own child's resistance indicates lack of interest in music. But, as we have already seen, this is not the case.

For a parent in the midst of daily battles with a child, it may be difficult to sympathize with those who complain that their child practices too much. But this phenomenon does exist and such self-motivated children create different challenges for their parents.

One father says that his over-achieving son Chris begins and ends every day with a practice session. Although Chris' father has tried to impose some limits on his son's rigid schedule, he has met with only partial success. Chris's self-discipline and intense drive worry his father, but Chris keeps insisting that he's fine.

Here's how one concerned parent, the mother of a high-school trumpeter in Pittsburgh, dealt with her son's over-intense practicing: she simply accepted it. She said that Jon knew when he wanted to practice. He had his own schedule. "Practice," she said, "always came before homework. I used to have a problem with that, but now I've just had to accept his priorities."

Parents who watch their children practice too much worry about their children's level of intensity. They worry that their children are overextending themselves, or not spending enough time with friends. They worry that all this practicing is affecting their children's health, or that the children are becoming high-strung perfectionists. Most of all, they worry that these children are not *normal*.

Other parents are not so much worried as confused. They don't understand what is making their children so stubborn and obsessive. These parents might be less concerned if they felt that their children were in good company, that there were others like them, and that they turned out alright. Take Kass, for instance, the conflicted high school student in Utah who simply loved playing the violin. Her mother was bewildered by it all:

> We have never, ever, asked Kass to practice...She set very high standards for herself and then got mad if she didn't perform up to them. She worked even harder the next time. When Kass was younger, I remember her waking early and practicing until I couldn't stand it any more. Once I interrupted her because we needed to run an errand. She continued to play until I was in the car and only then did she put her violin down and come out. When we got home from the errand and were getting out of the car, I heard the violin start up. Kass had already dashed into the house to resume her practicing! I don't know how she did it. I don't know where this drive came from. It sure didn't come from me.

Chapter Seven: Practice Makes Perfect

Some kids motivate themselves to practice through self-analysis. Joe, a cellist from Glendora, California, played with a youth orchestra, but was never disciplined about his music until he attended a summer program at the National Cello Institute. After his summer there, said his mother, grasping for words,

> he became like…well…not exactly obsessed, but…well, now he puts in between four and six hours of practice a day! And he judges himself after every practice. He will say, "Oh, that was a great practice." Or, "I just couldn't work through that passage very well." He's constantly analyzing what he's doing and he's always trying to make it better.

Joe had learned not only about music at his summer program, he also learned about *practicing* music, which had strengthened his interest and his level of understanding.

Some children display an uncanny focus and self-motivation even in kindergarten. That's how it was for Thomas, who grew up in Connecticut. His parents were not at all musical, but they noticed that Thomas was and so they started him on the piano. According to his father,

> Thomas never had to be told to practice. We worked on a schedule that allowed him to continue playing soccer and Little League Baseball. But even as a five-year-old, Thomas would come home from kindergarten, play the piano for 15 or 20 minutes, go and watch cartoons, and then come back to practice for another 15 minutes. He kept on doing that and, by the time the day was over, he had put in two hours—in kindergarten—just because he enjoyed it!

The father of Soovin, the professional violinist from New York, says his son was simply in love with the music; they "never once had to remind him or entice him to practice. What motivated him to practice with so much passion, even during his early childhood, seemed nothing but the music itself." This sounds romantic, but it is certainly the most profound reason to practice. And it is not uncommon. Indeed, as children continue with their music education, even those who were once openly rebellious may come to accept practicing because they have come to love the music.

The parents of the self-motivated children quoted above are not musicians, which may explain their sense of puzzlement. Parents who *are* musicians and have children who practice willingly understand this behavior in a different way. For them, it may be a given. A high-school orchestra teacher, the mother of a trombone player, explains that her daughter "practices every day now because she doesn't remember any time when she was not practicing. For her it's like eating or sleeping. No incentives are needed—it's just a part of her life."

Two Nebraska boys, whose father was a U.S. Air Force trumpeter, pushed their parents to let them play various brass instruments. Their mother says,

> We never told them they had to practice. They always enjoyed practicing. The boys were always pushing us, not the other way around. It was always, "Dad, show me this." Or "When can I get a C trumpet?" These children simply wanted to do what daddy did.

Andre Previn, pianist, composer, and conductor, explained that as a child growing up in a musical family, he practiced the piano for hours on end because he was naive. The poor child didn't know any better. He said, "Sometimes people ask me if I resented not having a normal childhood. I didn't know it wasn't normal. I thought everyone practiced eight hours a day." [44]

- **Teaching a Child How to Practice**

It is not generally known that children (as well as adults) have to be taught *how* to practice. It is not enough to say to a child, "Go and practice this." Does that mean to repeat something over and over? Sometimes, of course, that is exactly what it means, but even then, a student needs to learn how to make this repetition productive.

Chapter Seven: Practice Makes Perfect

The successful teacher explains what practicing means. The teacher should teach a child various practicing methods, for example breaking a large piece of music into small bites, playing the music extremely slowly, playing a difficult passage using various rhythmic values, and breathing properly.

There are many ways to show a child how to practice. One simple technique is a practice log or journal, where the child writes down, not just *what* he or she is practicing, but the *objective* of this practice session, and how the child will approach the task. At the end of a session, a student should list achievements, difficulties encountered, and areas that will need work in the next practice session. A log is invaluable as a record of how a student has used a practice session. The child becomes more conscientious and, most important, can see how effort and hard work have resulted in improvement. Ideally, the teacher will set up a system of record keeping for the child and will fill in some of the blanks before sending a student home.

- **Boring Scales and Exercises**

Good teachers today realize that they must combine exercises and scales with "easy little pieces" that are musically satisfying for beginners to play. I remember being amazed that my son's teacher, after only a few weeks of lessons, gave him a real piece of music. It was by Telemann and must have been extraordinarily easy to master. But the teacher had located excellent music that required only elementary skills. She was wise enough to know that the best way to keep the interest of her pupil was to give him real music to play.

So was the teacher of composer Darius Milhaud. Noting that his first violin teacher must have taught him well because his early lessons had *not* been boring, Milhaud wrote, "I had started to learn the violin when I was seven. When [my teacher] had taught me the elementary principles of the instrument, he made me read and play easy little pieces. He had realized from the outset that he would get nothing out of me by forcing me to do exercises that were too dull." [45]

Children hate practicing when it requires them to play boring scales and dull exercises. Noah, a 15-year-old Orlando violist, is typical. "He hates the drill work," says his mother. "Doing scales is torture. What he loves is sight reading and playing music with other kids. He balks at practicing, but he willingly plays the orchestral stuff and the solos." Or Jesse, a 17-year-old oboist from Oakland, who is "hard to get going if the piece doesn't appeal to him. If he's excited about a piece, though, he practices five days a week, up to two hours a day."

Well-known composers remember their tedious exercises with loathing. Wagner wrote of the piano lessons he endured in Leipzig, "the exercises soon filled me with great disgust owing to what I considered their dryness. For me music was demoniacal, a mystically exalted enormity: everything connected with rules seemed only to distort it." [46] Knowing how the great Richard Wagner remembers his piano exercises may help us feel more empathy for our own children's resistance to practicing scales.

But because they are the building blocks of musical expression, finger exercises are essential and scales must be mastered. As parents our task is to find ways to help our children practice, even as we sympathize with their resistance.

- **The Power of Group Music-Making**

Practicing music is a lonely activity. It is difficult for many adults to spend an hour alone in a room with nothing except their instrument. How much more difficult it is, then, for a child. But this is what is required to master an instrument. If children have the opportunity to play with others, however, they usually find a greater incentive to practice.

My son's flute teacher put her flute students into flute "choirs," or groups, each child playing a different part. She gave the group its chamber music lesson once a week when they came together to rehearse. There they learned to read music, to count rigorously, to listen carefully to one another, to laugh at their mistakes, and to high-five their successes. Their group lessons featured lots of silliness as well as serious music making. And at the end of the lesson, my son came home eager to practice his part because he couldn't let down the others in his group.

Educators know that children work more willingly when they actively engage in a group activity. Gone are the days when elementary-school children sat isolated all day at individual desks. Now, in most classrooms, children's desks are arranged for shared work and cooperative projects. Children have such a good time together that they often don't realize how much they are learning. Parents come into progressive schools like these and say, "It sure wasn't this much fun in school when *I* was a kid!"

Today's music educators also emphasize group music-making, placing children in small chamber music groups and youth orchestras that generate enthusiasm. Smart music teachers group their students into small clusters of two, three, or four for duets, trios and quartets. These teachers seek out music that is easy enough for their students to master, but challenging enough to be compelling. Children respond enthusiastically when taking music lessons is no longer so lonely. This is one strong argument for starting children on instruments other than the piano. The pianist usually plays alone, but a student playing an orchestral instrument is more likely to play with others, enjoy the experience, and continue to study music.

- **A Parent's Expectations**

Setting up clear expectations is a simple concept, but all too often parents with expectations fail to make them known to a child. They assume, often incorrectly, that the child knows what the parents' expectations are. By clearly stating what they expect, parents increase their chances for success. Marsha's young son was angry about practicing. Marsha, who is herself musical, was taking in his frustration and doing her best to listen with a sympathetic ear. The conversation went something like this:

Son: Mommy, I don't want to practice!

Mother: I understand you don't want to practice, but in our house we practice.

Son: Mommy, I just want to be good on my instrument.

Mother: Well, that's a good thing, but there's this catch to it. If you want to be good on your instrument, you have to practice.

Son: OK, OK, I'll practice.

Marsha added, "I know this sounds strange, but he finally got it. He simply hadn't seen the connection before." Marsha was amazed that such a simple conversation had had the effect it did. She claims that this was the turning point in her child's ability to accept his need to practice. Young children need repetition, not only on their instruments, but also on the connection between practicing and excellence. Parents can help children make that connection, but expectations need to be repeated as often as necessary (which is usually more often than parents think it should be).

The mother of Kate feels that parental expectations are key but are too seldom voiced with clarity. This mother often had to remind young Kate that practicing was expected of her. "No one is asking children if they want to study math or English, are they? It's just something they are expected to learn. So, if music is important to you, why not have similar expectations?" She explained that sometimes her daughter would protest and say, "I don't like the harp. It's ruining my life!" But her fits didn't last. They were emotional responses to fatigue, too much pressure, or not wanting to have such an unusual avocation. But her parents' expectations remained in place, Kate's negativity passed, and today she is a professional harpist in Virginia.

Parents must also set limits and explain what they will do, and what they expect their children to do. One Kentucky father told his daughter Valerie that they would drive her to her lessons and would

Chapter Seven: Practice Makes Perfect

pay for them, but that they expected her, in return, to practice. When she was 10 they were still on her case about practicing, but now that she's older "she doesn't need us to keep after her." Her father's clear messages helped assure the success of Valerie's musical studies.

Many children need help to start a practice session. One immigrant mother whose talented daughter plays the bassoon, says:

> Even though Mia is 14, I still have to initiate. I tell her, "Your time is now. You practice before homework." I make deals. I say, "What time do you want to do it? She says, "4:30." I say, "You have to stick with it." She makes all the excuses there are, especially, "I have to go bathroom." But now I tell her, "You go bathroom before you start practicing. I say, "One hour, sitting in the chair time." But once she sits down, she's OK. She just needs some help getting to the chair.

Many parents feel that unpleasantness needs to be avoided at all costs. The want peace in the house, and who doesn't? But accomplishing things usually means putting up with some degree of unpleasantness. Parents who can endure the difficult times, who can laugh them off instead of taking them too seriously, will have a stronger child who learns that the world will not come to an end if he or she is unhappy about having to do "work" and who, years later, will thank his or her parents for "making me practice."

- **Ways That Parents Can Help**

Parents can provide the obvious: a fixed practice time and a special practice place, with good lighting and a distraction-free environment. A fixed time usually works best because, without it, postponing practice is too easy. Parents can use encouraging language, renaming practice time "playing time." They can help young children divide their practice time into two shorter periods, or find CDs of the music their child is learning. The child can then play along or listen attentively. Parents (with the input of teachers) can suggest a variety of supplemental activities to "jazz up" a practice routine. Children can move their bodies to the music, dance to difficult rhythms, act out the music's emotional message, and use the music to compose lyrics or a story. A child can practice scales in a "funk" style or play a challenging passage backwards.

- **Being Present While a Child is Practicing**

Because practicing can be lonely, one of the best ways to help children establish a practice pattern or get through a difficult period is simply to sit with them. Being present reduces the loneliness factor. The mother of a high-school cellist from Pittsburgh said, "I practiced with Cecile for years. There were times when I just sat while she practiced. The great thing is that I don't have to do that any more. Now she is disciplined enough to do everything on her own."

Being present for practice is not a permanent commitment, as the mother of Michelle, an 18-year-old bassist from Louisville, explains:

> I have really battled with Michelle. Because practicing is so lonely, I tried to help her out by sitting at the piano and playing a few notes with her. My playing ability is not so hot though, and she would get impatient with me, but we just kind of muddled through things together. Sometimes I would just sit there while she worked on a difficult section. And then those times became fewer and fewer. Mostly because she was far ahead of me and I couldn't keep up with her musically, but also because she was more able to do it on her own.

The popular Suzuki method of teaching is based on parent participation and commitment. Parents attend music lessons, take notes, and practice with their children. The father of two violinists from Omaha, Nebraska, relished the Suzuki practice sessions with his two children. "We did a couple of Suzuki recitals when the three of us performed. I really enjoyed practicing with them." Not all parents, of course, will enjoy it. And not all parents can make such a serious commitment. But because their parents share their practicing, these students have fewer practice-time melt-downs.

- **Being Realistic**

Even with the best teaching, the best chamber music groups, and the best resources, many parents find it a challenge to maintain their child's practice schedule. Knowing that resistance to practicing is normal and that you are not alone in this, however, helps. The mother of a 17-year-old violinist has a realistic way of looking at the issue. Emily spends her summers at the Arrowbear Music Camp in the San Bernardino Mountains of Southern California. Her mother says:

> Unless your kid is a totally motivated genius, it's a question of work. I don't expect a kid to have the long-range vision that it takes to see that music is a goal worth attaining. Most kids want to play their instrument for a while, and then they discover that it's not always fun and that practicing involves a lot of repetition, and sometimes they don't feel like it. But I never expected Emily to be completely self-motivated. That's unrealistic. Many parents think that if kids say they are bored, then that's all there is to it. They think a kid should do what she wants to do all the time. If she doesn't want to practice, you shouldn't make her practice. But kids don't necessarily know what's good for them. If they say they don't like to eat vegetables, then they don't eat vegetables? Come on. Get real. Math skills are wonderful, they can make school easier for you and they can earn you a living. But music gives you something for *after* school, for your whole life.

This mother has a much better chance of success because she "never expected Emily to be self-motivated." Her clear understanding of the situation augurs well for her child's continuing success in music.

- **Logistics**

Establishing where and when to practice is a logistics issue which can be especially problematic where there is more than one child practicing in the house.

The Walkers of Illinois have three children who play instruments: trombone, French horn and bassoon. There aren't enough hours in the day or rooms in the house for all of their children's musical needs and sometimes there are conflicts. But they have worked out this arrangement: one goes downstairs to the family room, one goes to the living room, and one practices in his bedroom where he has territorial rights. All three children like the living room best because there's a piano and a metronome there, but whoever gets there first gets to practice there. The house sometimes sounds like a concert hall when the orchestra is tuning up.

The Murphys also have three children who practice their instruments in a house no bigger than 1200 square feet. Their mother says,

> How do we manage it? Neal comes into my bedroom, shuts the door and practices the flute. Jarrod comes into my office, shuts the door and practices the trumpet, and Hope plays her violin in the living room where there isn't a door to shut. Somehow it works.

The Marshalls have three daughters who all play the harp. "There's only one harp for the three girls," their mother says, "but they practice at different times. One practices at night. One practices after school. The third one doesn't practice much at all."

- **Incentives and Rewards**

Psychologists know how to shape both animal and human behavior by offering rewards and punishments. Although this idea has become a cliché, it is still worth noting because it is crucial: rewarded behavior tends to continue while behavior that is punished tends to decrease. We parents can help our children accept the demands of music practicing by offering incentives to shape their behavior. Just as teachers use stickers to reinforce positive behaviors in students, parents can offer their own motivators.

If a child's teacher does not create a practice log, a parent can help the child make one and use it to record his minutes of practice. Even better, parents can reward a child's practicing when pre-set goals are met. Some high school orchestras use students' practice logs to give them academic credit, a very powerful, real, and tangible reward.

Chapter Seven: Practice Makes Perfect

Food is a classic reward. One mother gives her young violinist daughter a grape for each repetition of a tedious passage. Five-year-old Antonio has a mother who puts M&M's on the piano keys and lets him eat one only after he hits the correct key.

There are other techniques worth trying. The mother of a violist says, "We've done the charts with the little stars. Most of our stuff, though, is by the stopwatch. The watch doesn't lie. When Jim's practicing, the stop watch is on. He's off into La La Land a lot, so the watch really helps." The mother of a violinist says,

> We ran into lots of practicing issues. But we just plowed on. Sometimes when Kate didn't want to be indoors, we would take the music stand outside and practice on the driveway. Sometimes, when Kate said she was too tired, we would lie down on the rug and practice. The important thing for us was to persist.

Parents offer rewards all too seldom, given how effective rewards can be. Some parents fear that their children will learn to work only for the reward. But this is rarely the case. We are talking here about offering rewards (even if you think of them as bribes) as a temporary, stop-gap measure, not as a way of life. If practicing is not fun, parents can help find a way to make it more fun, or at least tolerable. One mother sees bribery as a way of getting past the bumps. She says,

> OK, you want a Nintendo game? Fine. Now if you practice this much in three months, we'll do that. I'd just incorporate whatever her goal was. Sometimes it was an activity, going to a park. With my daughter it was buying her a new T-shirt. Bribery works.

When Maurice Ravel, the French composer, was only seven years old, his parents used positive reinforcement to get past the bumps in his practice road. They used a standard reward that adults go for, too: money. According to his biographer,

> Ravel was never a very diligent piano pupil, even as a student at the Conservatoire, but far from bullying him into practicing at this early stage, his parents payed (sic) him six sous for every

> half hour he put in—which compares not at all badly with the fifty centimes his teacher received for the same amount of tuition. He apparently needed no such inducement to work when, in 1887, he started studying harmony, counterpoint, and composition.[47]

The money reward helped Ravel overcome his resistance, but he later did the work for its own sake. Do not fear that you will need to continue the bribery forever or that you will turn your child into a young mercenary. Use what works.

Money is a powerful motivator. It is what motivates adults to get up every morning and to go to work. More than one parent makes a child's allowance dependent on sufficient practice time. But money can be, and is, often used in a more subtle way. Parents often remind their children about the cost of their music lessons. If the child is old enough and sassy enough, he or she may respond with "Don't lay a guilt trip on me." But a little guilt, artfully applied, can be a very effective motivator. It certainly motivates us as adults in ways too common to mention.

One parent used this highly unusual system:

> After every lesson, my child's teacher reported on the quality of the lesson. If Karen had prepared enough and the lesson was a good one, I would pay for the lesson, but if she had *not* prepared well enough, then *she* had to pay for the lesson. That kid learned to practice real fast. Kids just have no idea of what it means to drop $45 every Monday night for a lesson. If the lesson isn't worthwhile, you've just flushed that money down the toilet.

An Anaheim grandmother was sacrificing a lot to raise her grandson Nick. She nevertheless strongly encouraged his experiments with saxophone, flute, oboe, clarinet, and trombone. When his grandmother began paying for private piano lessons however, she insisted that Nick practice piano, his primary instrument, explaining,

> If you pay for lessons you have to practice. Nick was very frugal himself and he understood about not wasting money.

> He never wanted me to buy him anything he didn't need. He would say, "Save your money, Gramma, I don't really need that." So he understood the relationship between paying for lessons and practicing. He wanted me to get my money's worth.

The mother of Lina, a 13-year-old cellist, reports that Lina and her other three children practice willingly for at least an hour a day. Lina's parents have made their expectations and their financial situation clear to their children. Lina's mother says,

> We have a rule in our family. Because this is a financial struggle for us. Our rule has always been that we are happy to pay for the lessons, but once we do that, the children need to do their part. So we haven't had too much of a problem, because the kids realize that practicing is part of the deal.

Children who know that their family is sacrificing to give them music lessons (or any other "extra"), feel more gratitude for the indulgence and are more likely to reciprocate by doing what is expected of them. This may be one of those rare situations where having less money is better than having more.

- **The Middle School Years**

This is a fairly typical pattern: enthusiasm and willingness to practice when the child is young; foot-dragging and outright rebellion in the middle school years; followed by a more mature approach to practicing in high school. Young children may love to perform for admirers and they may practice happily. But when they get older, they are not so cute. There comes that time when they no longer want to practice. This can be anytime, of course, but it most often occurs around the middle school years, or when they are between 12 and 15 years old. It was when he was 12 that my son and I had our futile shouting match about who would call the teacher to tell her that he was quitting. By the end of high school, however, Jonathan was practicing independently.

Virginia's daughter fell in love with the harp when she was in first grade. Her mother remembers:

> After we got her that harp, she practiced all the time. She practiced from then until she was 12 without being reminded. After her 12th birthday it took lots of reminders to get her going. But now that she is finishing high school and thinking about college, she is back to practicing a lot, especially when she's got performances coming up.

Will, a clarinetist from a small town in Pennsylvania, became recalcitrant about practicing in 6th grade. His mother says,

> I had to cajole him, saying, "Come on, I'm paying for these lessons! Can you practice at least enough to be prepared for your lessons?" But now that he is finishing high school, practicing has just become a natural part of his life. Somewhere along the way he became impassioned. Then he was living and breathing music.

So what happens to students during their middle school years? Well, for one thing they want to be just like the cool kids, and the cool kids may not be carrying violin cases. A Houston mother explains:

> Sam was so worried about being cool that he refused to take his violin to school. We had to have one violin at home and another one at school so he wouldn't have to be seen carrying that case! The orchestra teacher was not keen on this arrangement, but I felt it could work. Let them get through these years any way they can. So for three years during middle school he rode the bus to school every day without the violin. Later when he got to high school, he grew out of that self-consciousness and was willing to carry the violin case again! He played soccer and he also played violin. He just decided he was a cool guy and he figured he could do anything he wanted to do and still be cool.

It takes considerable understanding for parents to make it through these years, and not just in terms of music. It helps if parents know the territory of youth, perhaps by remembering their life at that age. Vicky was a talented cellist who didn't want to practice the cello during her middle-school years. She explored dance, sports, and theater, wanting to find her "own thing." Luckily she was blessed with a mother who was a professional violinist and who understood

Chapter Seven: Practice Makes Perfect

how her daughter was feeling when she resisted practicing. How did her mother know? Because Mom had felt the same way when she was in junior high school! Her mother said,

> I was one of those kids who didn't want to practice myself. That's why I knew not to quit Vicky's lessons when she stopped practicing. When I entered junior high, I was embarrassed to be seen with a violin in school. That violin made me feel like an outsider. I grew up in Long Beach where there were few musicians in my school. I mean, the kids looked at me like I was from another planet. With my violin case, there was no way I could be cool and hip.

Since Vicky's mother remembered her own self-conscious youth, she allowed her daughter to get through those difficult years and to continue taking music lessons, even though she was barely practicing. She felt that Vicky would probably come back to music, just as she herself had done when she was Vicky's age. And she was right. After majoring in music at UCLA, Vicky became a professional cellist.

When Aaron reached middle school and resisted practicing the piano, his mother decided to think of his weekly piano lesson as simply "time for music." It was the one time in the week when Aaron sat and talked about music and theory and improvisation. He loved the lessons minus the practicing. Aaron's mother felt that it wasn't necessary for him to practice in order to have the privilege of music lessons. She let him continue like this until he was 14. Aaron never really took to the piano, but he did become an oboist and majored in oboe performance at the University of Michigan.

When a child loses interest in practicing, particularly if it occurs around the middle school years, it may just be a predictable stage that needs to be lived through. But it could also be an indication of a particular issue that needs serious attention. It may be that the music assigned the child is no longer challenging. That was the problem for Rachel, a horn player from the Detroit area. According to her mother,

> Once Rachel decided she had mastered something, ennui set in. In high school, the music itself was not challenging enough for her so, though she would practice for her lessons, she was easily distracted by the phone or a TV show. I remember her starting the clock by playing for a couple of minutes and then setting the horn down to talk on the telephone and then, 20 minutes later, picking up the horn again and announcing that her half hour was finished.

In this case, the solution was to upgrade the level of music that Rachel was being assigned by her high school orchestra teacher. In other cases, the issue may be that a child has "outgrown" a teacher. Although this is not usually the case, if practicing languishes, it could be time to consider changing teachers. (We will look at issues involving private teachers in the next chapter.)

- **Quitting**

Few adults ever complain that their parents made them study music, but many people do complain that their parents didn't make them practice enough. Even professional musicians reminiscing about their childhoods express regret about not practicing more. Joan Sutherland's father had died when she was young and her mother struggled to pay for Joan's early piano lessons. "I was told there'd be no more if I didn't do what Miss Juncker required. Foolish child that I was, I continued to play what I wanted and have regretted it ever since, as Mother kept her word and the piano lessons stopped." [48]

But what is a parent to do when his child wants to quit, not only practicing, but also taking music lessons? I came perilously close to experiencing this. One grown woman, a professional violinist today, remembers with gratitude that her "mother 'used good psychology' on me. She said, 'OK, you want to quit, you can quit, but just continue it for one more year.' She very cleverly got me past that one really bad year." So one way to succeed as a parent is just to hold on by holding out. Undermine the child's resentment about having to continue by agreeing to allow him or her to quit, but stretch out the quitting date. Often, at the end of that period of time, the child will have grown past the resentment and will continue music lessons more willingly.

In another story featuring inadvertent "reverse psychology," Shana's mother reports that Shana once staged an adolescent rebellion over practicing. Her mother, exhausted, decided to cave in and stop giving Shana violin lessons.

> Right after Shana had chosen her audition piece for the orchestra she wanted to get into, she said she wanted to quit. I lost it. It was very ugly. Shana stormed off and I stormed off too. Fifteen minutes later, the next thing I know, she throws this note down on the kitchen table. It says, "You just want me to quit lessons so that I can't get into the orchestra, and you are so mean, and I am not going to quit, because I am going to play in the orchestra next year whether you want me to or not!"

Aren't adolescents wonderful? In the heat of the tumult they engender, we parents have to remember that they are adolescents!

A grandmother raising her grandson, Cameron, tells this second-chance story. She had made the mistake of allowing her daughter, Cameron's mother, to quit taking music lessons. But she was more experienced "the second time around." When raising her grandson, she handled it differently:

> Cameron really wanted to take violin until he found out he had to practice. Then he wasn't all that gung-ho. So I had to stay on top of him about practicing. Now that he's played for a while, I only have to remind him sometimes, and he's in there practicing. If I had let him, though, he would have quit years ago when he found out that he had to practice. I told him, "You asked for the violin, you have to learn to play it. If, after you learn the instrument, you want to quit, then that's OK, but not until you learn it well." I decided on this approach because a generation ago I had let my daughter stop her music lessons the very first time she wanted to quit and now she really regrets it. But I got a second chance raising my grandson and I'm not making that same mistake twice.

Of course, when a child masters an instrument, he or she has achieved excellence and is much less likely to abandon his pursuit. That's what the Walkers believe. They say that all of their children practiced willingly for the first year but each of them reached a point where they lost their enthusiasm and thought about quitting. This period lasted from six months to a year. But the parents told them, "Music is something important. Let's work through it." They helped by assigning specific times for their practicing. Gradually, the children started seeing results and they sounded good to themselves. As their son Thomas later said, "I found out that the more I practiced, the better I sounded, and the better I sounded, the more I liked to play. It made me feel like I could do anything I set my mind to." What a side benefit of practicing—to learn that hard work will bring you results!

- **Where Credit Is Due**

There are many artists who, as adults, give credit to their parents for insisting that they practice. The renowned New Zealand soprano, Kiri Te Kanawa, said, "Looking back on it now I can see Mummy constantly kept the music going. I'd tend not to feel like it because I was a lazy child, but she'd insist that I sang." [49] Marilyn Horne said "the lessons my dad taught me have stood me in good stead for nearly half a century…I wouldn't be singing today if I hadn't stuck to the principles [of practicing] established by my father." [50] And Pablo Casals, the great cellist, said, "If it hadn't been for my mother's conviction and determination that music was my destiny, it is quite conceivable that I'd have become a carpenter. But I do not think I would have made a very good one." [51]

CHAPTER EIGHT

PRIVATE TEACHERS

If your child is learning to play an instrument in a school orchestra, there will inevitably come a time when you start thinking about private lessons. Other parents, players, or teachers may speak to you about private lessons, or your child may ask for them. Why should anyone whose child is studying music at school undertake additional outside lessons?

No matter how talented and dedicated the school music teacher is, he cannot devote an entire hour of the day to your child. Even if he could, he is not likely to be an expert on your child's instrument because, to teach orchestra or band, he is required to have only rudimentary knowledge about each instrument. A child who begins to play an instrument without proper instruction, using incorrect fingering for example, may never be able to overcome "wrong habits" and, as a result, will fail to achieve excellence on an instrument.

"I only wish I had found a better teacher for the early years," is a familiar refrain heard from parents who, for one reason or another, didn't give their children private lessons as beginners. Living in the mountains of North Carolina, the mother of a pianist said that she couldn't find her son a well qualified private teacher until he was in sixth grade. She said, "I'm afraid he could have gained a lot more than he did in those early years. I didn't understand then how important a musical foundation was."

What private teachers give children is instruction at exactly the required level—no time is wasted. They provide correct technique, appropriately challenging material, and a powerful boost in children's drive, self-confidence, and level of performance. A private teacher motivates. Parents report that, with a good private teacher, their children's interest and performance level "take off," often dramatically.

- **Finding a Private Teacher**

How does one find a good private teacher? The obvious answer is to ask the people who are most likely to know. Ask the music teachers at your child's school for their recommendations. If you meet parents who rave about their child's teacher, corner them. Music store employees are good referral sources, and some music stores have lists of teachers they can recommend. You can also find teachers advertising in local papers—and some of them have degrees from respected conservatories. You can also consult local colleges, schools of music, the Young Musicians Foundation, the Music Teachers of America, and various web sites.

Ask questions of prospective teachers and check their backgrounds. If possible, attend a recital and talk to the teacher's students. This will give you a good idea of the kind of students who study with that teacher. If teachers will allow it, watch them give a lesson. This is an excellent way to judge their professionalism, teaching style, and emotional involvement with their students.

Chapter Eight: Private Teachers

The important thing is to find the teacher who is right for *your* child. Do not grab the first acceptable teacher who comes your way. Take your time to find the right one. You are going to be seeing this person a lot, you are going to be paying for his professional services over an extended period of time, and your child is likely to develop a real relationship with him.

When a violinist's family from Connecticut moved to California, it took them a year to find a teacher with whom they felt satisfied. The first teacher wasn't challenging, and the second one slapped their child's hands, but the third teacher was a gem.

Certainly do not make the decision about teachers based on convenience. The best teachers are least likely to be willing to come to your house.

You should find a teacher that both you and your child "click" with— a comfortable personality match is an important factor in assuring a good fit. Try out four or five teachers before you make your final selection. Explain that you are in the process of choosing a teacher and ask for a "trial lesson." Some teachers give free trial lessons, but most do not and will ask to be compensated for their time, which is only fair. If the teacher bristles at being "auditioned," that can help you make a decision. At the end of the first lesson, your child should have learned something and should be able to tell you what he or she learned.

Don't be afraid to ask questions when you interview a prospective teacher. The Music Teachers National Association suggests the following questions which you can use as a loose guide for asking your own:

1. What is your professional experience in music?

2. What is your teaching experience? What age groups do you teach?

3. How do you participate in ongoing professional development?

4. Are you nationally certified by the Music Teachers National Association?

5. Do you have a written policy? Will you review it with me?

6. Do you regularly evaluate student progress?

7. What instructional materials do you use?

8. What kinds of music do you teach?

9. What other elements do you use as a part of your teaching curriculum?

10. Do you offer group lessons?

11. Do you require students to perform in studio recitals during the year?

12. Do you offer other performance opportunities for your students, such as festivals and competitions?

13. Do you use technology in your studio, such as computers, music instruction software, and digital keyboards?

14. How much practice time do you require each day?

15. What do you expect of your students? What do you expect of their parents?

A word about the term "studio." When I first heard it, I imagined a wood-paneled room replete with Oriental carpets, old-world paintings, and ornate music stands. But in this context the word "studio" is not a room at all. It refers to the collection of students that a private teacher teaches. The room in which a person teaches can be plain-vanilla ordinary, cluttered with personal papers, pretentiously appointed, light and airy, or heavy and dark. But don't be overly influenced by the setting—you are there for the instruction, not the décor.

Even after selecting a teacher, you are not committed for life. See how it goes and use your child's attitude and progress as your guide. You may need to continue with that teacher for a month or two before being confident that this is the right teacher for your child.

One indication of a successful teacher is that there is a "waitlist." This attests to the popularity of the teacher, and there is usually a good reason for popularity. You can have your name added to the waitlist while you are considering other teachers or you may decide to start with another teacher while waiting for an opening in a sought-after teacher's studio.

Reputation and popularity, however, are not infallible indicators of a teacher's excellence. A famous musician with a large following can be disastrous as a teacher. Just as there are professors who are renowned for their brilliant contributions to science but cannot make their thoughts intelligible to undergraduates, so there are brilliant violinists who wow the crowds with their virtuosity, but cannot easily explain to a student how to hold a bow.

If your child is technically advanced and serious about music, you should consider taking him or her to the very best teacher, which often means one of the best performers in your area. Who are they? The best performers are found in the top orchestras, and the orchestra's best performer in each instrumental group is the "principal," the one who performs the solo parts in symphonic concerts.

Orchestral musicians often teach, but usually they teach only advanced high school or college students. Explore this possibility, because the fact that your teacher performs and you can go to hear her and see her on stage is a powerful motivator for students. Again the caveat: not all good players are good teachers, but when your teacher can tell you stories about the funny personality quirks of last night's famous conductor, it does add excitement and glamour to weekly lessons.

Professional teachers charge serious money, and teachers in large metropolitan areas charge most. Members of the best orchestras, for example the New York or Los Angeles Philharmonic, are well paid, and yet many of them take on private students for the challenge, the satisfaction, and of course, for the extra income. Professional musicians of this caliber may charge more than $100 an hour, but these fees reflect their qualifications as performers more than as teachers. It is a good idea to "audition" these top musicians just as carefully as you would as any other teacher.

- **The Teen-Age Teacher**

If your child is a beginner, you have the option of choosing a young, inexpensive, and convenient teacher. The least expensive teachers are talented middle and high-school students whose youthful informality makes them appealing to many children. A 13-year old is too young to work in construction or in a sales job, but not too young to teach music, especially if he or she is a talented flutist who likes children. Not just any 13-year old flutist will do, however, even for a raw beginner. Be sure that this teenager is *currently* taking professional lessons, and that his professional teacher is willing to serve as a "mentor" for the "student teacher." Ask for both teachers' names and numbers and do a "background check." Like the professionals, young people *must* be tried out—some can teach and some cannot. If you are able to tell the difference, you can get a real bargain here.

To find a good teen-age teacher, ask your local public and private schools for recommendations. Some professional teachers will agree to send one of their capable students to coach a beginner, especially if their own studio is full.

The advantages of using a high-school or a college student can be seductive: these young teachers are relatively inexpensive and arrangements are easy to make. A youngster will often charge $15 an hour and think that's a great deal. Whereas the busy professional

Chapter Eight: Private Teachers

musician will almost never come to your house, the teenager may be happy to bike on over.

Many teachers and music educators feel strongly that a beginner on any instrument should be taught only by a professional. They have good reasons for their opinion: they will have to pick up where the amateurs left off. They inherit all the incorrect finger or mouth positions and fumbling that the inexperienced teenage teacher didn't, couldn't, or (more often) wouldn't correct.

These young, inexperienced teachers may know how to play, but not know how to communicate their knowledge. In any field of endeavor, beginners imitate their teachers imperfectly. (That's the nature of a beginner.) Minor differences accumulate and build into finger or mouth habits that can impede further progress. Young teachers who recognize these problems may lack the experience to offer solutions. Most often, however, the problem is not their inability to correct students—it is their unwillingness. They too are young and want to be liked. They hesitate to correct their young students and they back off from insisting. They may lack the maturity to see past the moment, and they may not know how to "push" or challenge their young charges.

When it works, however, finding a talented teenager to teach your kids can be a real coup. The mother of a 13-year-old teacher proudly affirms: "My daughter's nine-year-old students love her just like she loved her beginning teen-age teacher. She charges them $5 for a half hour and pockets her spending money for the week." Even as an imperfect teacher, if the teenager loves music and conveys that love, he or she can nurture the beginner and prepare the child for studying with a professional.

- **The Right Professional Teacher**

Puccini, the great opera composer, was first taught piano by his uncle who informed Puccini's mother, after several unproductive lessons, that the boy had no talent. When his mother heard this, she promptly found her son a different teacher. The boy fell in love both with the new teacher and with music and quickly became a fine pianist.[52] We are left to wonder whether the world would have been deprived of *La Boheme* without the determination of Puccini's mother.

The Puccinis' experience demonstrates the importance of a good fit between teacher and student. A fearful child will do best with a teacher whose approach is non-threatening, and who offers group recitals where children play trios and quartets rather than heart-thumping solos. One child responds best to humor, another to challenge. One child may require structured exercises; another, hang-loose explorations. One student needs patience, while another responds best to demands. A good teacher knows which approach is called for and when to use it. The mother of a violinist praised her daughter's teacher, saying, "My child's teacher is demanding but he's like a fisherman—he knows when to tighten the line and also when to relax it when the fish is struggling."

Most children respond best to warmth and encouragement, but other children require a certain distance, or formality, in order to make progress. If a child finds he or she can do little and still get a pat on the back, the child may lose respect for the teacher and lose interest in the music. On the other hand, if a tough teacher takes on a tough kid, a contest of wills can ensue, leading to an unpleasant and unproductive power struggle. For progress and success to occur, the one with the power needs to be the teacher. Of course, it goes without saying that the teacher's power should be appropriate—the kind that empowers students.

Since teachers come in all gradations, it's important to find one whose standards and personality match your child's particular needs.

- **The Good Teacher**

A "good" teacher is one who can effectively—verbally and physically—communicate with students. If a child cannot produce the correct tone and is simply told to "try harder," he or she may become frustrated and feel humiliated. The teacher's job is to show physically and explain verbally *how* to produce that tone.

The teacher must be able not only to gauge a child's level, but also to assign material that will challenge the child without overwhelming her. Material too advanced will discourage children; material too easy will bore them. If exercises are not musically interesting, they will not engage the student. Exercises are essential for the fingers, but real music grabs the heart.

Some overly ambitious parents, grooming their talented children towards a career in performing, attend local competitions to see which teachers produce the winners. On the basis of these "wins," they decide who the "best" teachers are. Beware. Yes, this can be a way of determining which teachers are coaching some of the most talented local young musicians, but that does not mean that their teaching *created* the talent. Equally talented youngsters may *not* be competing because their teachers wisely feel their students are not yet ready for it, or because they fear that the competition itself is a distraction. Worse, for some children, competition can be discouraging, can dampen enthusiasm, and can "burn out" young talent. This is a well known phenomenon.

- **Travel**

To a busy parent who gets home late from work, a teacher who comes to the house sounds like just the ticket. The neighborhood teacher, a block away, sounds like heaven on earth. If you find a good teacher next door, this can be a godsend, but if you are considering your child's education, be prepared to travel. Parents whose children are serious about music typically drive—a lot.

The mother of a Washington, D.C. high-school harpist took her daughter once a month to the renowned Curtis Institute of Music in Philadelphia.

> It was a three-hour drive, one-way! I would have thought that a person who did that was crazy! But that was before the harp. Once, when it snowed 30 inches in Philly, we had to take the train. My daughter wouldn't think of missing her lesson. Can you imagine tramping through the snow with a harp?

A father who moved frequently with his family reported that the distances he traveled to reach his child's music teachers varied. "In Ann Arbor, the teacher was five minutes away, in Maryland, 15 minutes, and in Africa, five hours."

My own son's first teacher lived only 10 minutes from our house, but his second teacher was an hour's drive away and she could be reached only by car. Until Jonathan was 16 and could drive, I spent the better part of every Saturday driving there, waiting through the lesson, and driving home. Stopping after the lesson for a little lunch somewhere, just the two of us, gave me "quality time" with Jonathan, but nevertheless "the music lesson" took up a major chunk of our family's weekend.

- **Dedication, Generosity, and Authority**

Making sacrifices of time and money, parents expect reciprocation from their children. They expect their child to learn a lot and to submit to the considerable authority of the teacher. "Do what the teacher says," is a common refrain from parents.

"Mama, I don't see why we have to stand with our feet like this," complained a young violin student about his teacher's requirement. "Can't we stand with our feet in another way? I look at people in orchestras and they don't even *stand*. They sit. I want to sit and be comfortable, too." This mother told her son, "At home, you can sit if you want, but in the lessons, you have to do exactly what the teacher says."

The private teacher demands from a student, and is given, true authority. One mother marveled that her child's cello teacher "could tell him to brush his teeth every night and, for *her*, he would!"

Teachers ask for commitment, sometimes for total commitment. A violin teacher in Seattle refused to take on one student until she had interviewed him and asked, "Are you going to practice? Are you going to listen to me?" Right from the start, this boy knew what his

Chapter Eight: Private Teachers

teacher's expectations were, and he knew he had to meet her high standards.

In high school, my son wanted to go on a summer-abroad program, which would have meant giving up his flute lessons for two months. He consulted his teacher about it. Her response: "Do you want to fish or cut bait?" He worried about what that meant for a week and then told her he wanted to fish. He resigned himself to staying home practicing that summer and took not one, but two lessons a week. He would meet her demands if meeting them was required to become a professional flutist.

Teachers who make demands on behalf of the student's best interests are often also dedicated and extremely generous. When my son's teacher gave him those two lessons a week, she charged us for only one hour of her time. Another mother found that, when her son started studying with the principal chair of the Phoenix Symphony, after the agreed-upon, one-hour lesson the man talked to her son for another hour—and sometimes two—giving the boy sound information and helpful guidance. A Chicago mother said that her son's violin teacher gave his student a "million-dollar lesson that lasted twice as long as we paid for. Sometimes longer."

The immigrant mother of a violinist was amazed at the attitude her son's teacher expressed.

> The teacher tells me, "I talk a lot, but I charge you only when we play, not when we talk...I make a pretty good living. Teaching is not the way I make money. I have only eight students and I only teach the ones I like." And I say to myself, maybe she's just trying to be nice, but this continues for two and a half years. On and on and on, for a lot over the hour. She says, "No, no, no, I'm just happy to teach him."

This mother felt enormous appreciation for the teacher's generosity and dedication to her son.

- **Does Private Mean "No Parent Welcome"?**

Should you, the parent, be present at your child's lessons? The Suzuki method of teaching requires parent participation, but many teachers feel that a parent's presence divides the child's concentration. Some teachers feel uncomfortable being so closely observed.

It is helpful to be present initially in order to gauge your child's comfort level, but if the child objects or is uneasy in your presence, by all means respect those feelings. Learning an instrument involves making mistakes, and many children are embarrassed to make mistakes in front of their parents. They can learn much more easily when they don't have an "audience" to observe their difficulties.

- **Teacher-Student Bonds**

The relationship between students and private teachers resonates with intellectual, artistic, and emotional depth. Because the relationship rests on understanding and interpreting music, it has an intellectual component. Because it concerns making and performing music, it has an artistic component. Because the private teacher-student bond is a one-on-one relationship and because musicality calls forth feelings, the bond between teacher and student is deeply emotional. Unlike the one-year relationship between a student at school and a favorite teacher, the ties with a student's private teacher last for several years. This extended time together can deepen the emotional bond significantly.

If private teachers become emotionally connected to their students and the families of their students, the teacher may at times fill the role of counselor, therapist, or may even become like extended family. The mother of a bassist blesses her daughter's teacher for helping her daughter "through the hormonal years."

> There were times when the man just let her cry through her lessons! She was frustrated by things having nothing to do with music, and there he was, listening to her, sympathizing with her, and seeing her through it.

Chapter Eight: Private Teachers

The father of a violinist shook his head in wonder and appreciation, recalling that his son's teacher was "like another grandmother" to him. One cellist's father says that his son thinks of his teacher as a big sister who throws great parties and lets him come to them. A flutist's mother says that her daughter's teacher has "become part of our family now. We've watched her get married and have two babies!"

These teachers may become such a part of the family that the relationship can extend well past the lesson-giving years. Daniel's trumpet teacher goes to all of his former student's concerts, as well as their soccer matches. Even though Daniel now studies with the symphony orchestra's principal trumpeter, his old teacher invites Daniel and his family to cook outs and they include him in their family bike rides. A harpist's teacher moved back to his native England, but stayed in touch with his former student's family for years. When the family vacationed one year in England, they were all invited to his home for afternoon tea.

- **Reasons for Changing Teachers**

The most common reason for a student to switch teachers is that the child needs a new challenge or a different technique.

When beginning students reach a more sophisticated level, their teachers (many of whom specialize in teaching beginners) suggest they move on to a teacher whose area of expertise is working with advanced students. Sometimes a child's first private teacher is such a warm, familiar figure that the child becomes too comfortable, and loses respect for the teacher's demands. Sometimes the child "outgrows" the teacher or stops enjoying lessons. One Los Angeles mother says that when she saw her son was no longer enjoying his cello and wanted to give it up, she went to the Colburn School of Music and asked for "someone fun." She credits that new someone with saving her son's love for music.

How long should a child study with a teacher? As a general rule, for three or four years. After that period of time, the child or young adult has learned the essence of what any one teacher can provide. Just as elementary school students learn different things from their fifth and sixth grade teachers, the music student needs to be exposed to multiple pedagogues and differing styles.

What are the signs that a student may need to change teachers? If a child who shows musical promise has become "stuck," has hit a plateau, loses interest, or resists practicing more than usual, it is time to seriously consider a change. This is not a criticism of the teacher. It simply means that the child has grown and may benefit from a fresh approach.

Ideally, the teacher and student should decide together that the time has come for the student to move on. The first teacher then recommends to the student someone who would best serve the student's needs, and the teacher makes the initial inquiries and introductions. This is the ideal, and is what happened with my son. When Jonathan and his teacher decided he needed a new flute teacher, his first teacher had strong feelings about who would be best for him and insisted that he go only to this teacher. Although I was skeptical and hated the hour's drive each way, the new teacher was clearly the right choice for my son, and we could never have found her on our own.

Another parent told this story of the process by which a change of teachers took place:

> When Avi felt he needed a new piano teacher, he spoke with his first teacher and, though it was hard for both teacher and student, they worked it out to their satisfaction. The first teacher arranged for him to meet with two teachers at different universities and to make a selection between them.

Some teachers encourage their students to experience other teachers as a way to develop the student's skills. A New York father felt fortunate to have his son study with such a teacher.

> He encouraged my son to interact with a variety of other musicians and teachers through youth orchestras, chamber music groups, and summer camps. He felt that the boy's

musical development would be enhanced by exposure to a wide range of different styles and interpretations and that having only one teacher would not provide this.

- **Issues in Changing Teachers**

The mother of a violinist reported that there was a protocol for changing from one teacher to another, and that it was a challenging experience:

> When we lived in Washington, D.C., we had to follow a grandfather code of ethics: the proper way to switch was to talk to the current teacher about the idea before making an appointment with another teacher. We needed to get the "permission" from the current teacher first. But it was difficult to get an agreement from Nicolas' teacher to look for a different teacher after he had been with her for five years.

One challenge in changing teachers is the sense of mutual attachment. This kind of healthy attachment is a powerful motivator for a child learning music. It is natural for a child to love a teacher, and the desire to learn is enhanced by a deep personal relationship.

Most students say that changing teachers is emotionally draining. To ease the transition, some students try studying with the old and the new teacher simultaneously. When my son was feeling distressed about leaving his first, much-loved teacher, we tried to retain her, but she refused to be a part of his "clinging" to her, as she said. She thought that it would only confuse Jonathan and that he would do better to make a clean break. But other teachers allow concurrent studying with a second teacher. A cellist who wanted to change teachers was told by his current teacher that he could get coaching from teachers he thought might be suitable for the future, but that she should continue to be his "home" teacher. The mother said,

> We did as the teacher specified, and the following year we changed his cello teacher to one of the ones he had taken lessons with. It took us one year to make the switch, but it wasn't a bad way of doing it.

Describing how her violist son changed teachers, one mother said,

> Eventually we found a new teacher, but we couldn't give up the old teacher! So we kept on going to two teachers a week—one for the old emotional stuff and one for the new technical stuff. I guess we were doing as much therapy as music, but it worked.

Some students are unnerved by having to leave their teacher. "My son was so loyal to his clarinet teacher that he couldn't bear to hurt his feelings," said one Pennsylvania mother. "So when he started studying with the new teacher, he simply wasn't able to tell his first teacher about it. He went on like this for months, feeling shame, remorse, and real conflict."

It is also not hard to see why a teacher may become attached to a student. As healthy and productive as their attachment may have been, it can make it difficult for the teacher to "lose" a student to someone else. The difficulty may increase when a child shows musical promise, because the student's accomplishments are the teacher's as well. Although it is certainly not true of most teachers, some who lose a student feel betrayed. They have given this child the best they had to offer, shared their hard-won knowledge and secrets, initiated him into the society of musicians, taught him the tricks of the trade, supported him when he was down, cheered for him when he was up. The teacher justifiably feels that she is responsible for the musical success the child has enjoyed. And now, when the student has reached this level of excellence, now...the child is abandoning the teacher, throwing him or her out for a newer model?

The teacher's feeling of betrayal is captured in a story told by a harpist. Her teacher had suggested that Barbara move on to a new teacher and, when Barbara followed her advice, the teacher became resentful, and said, "You're going to go *there*?" Rationally, the teacher knew that Barbara needed to move on, but emotionally the teacher was attached to her and felt abandoned when Barbara agreed to make the change. This kind of ambivalence is akin to what is felt by the mother proudly walking her three-year old to nursery school and then quietly crying when the child is happy to stay at school without her.

In addition to the stress felt by both student and teacher, this transition can also be difficult for the parents. There is something intense about the relationship you as a parent develop with someone who is teaching your child for years. The teacher is more than just a friend of the family—it's almost as if he or she has come into your family and has helped you to raise this child. If a teacher drops out of the life of the child and the family, it can feel traumatic for everyone. If the old teacher feels hurt and withdraws, other family members feel a sense of loss as well.

A mother told this story with glistening eyes and a trembling voice:

> My daughter Kelly had studied oboe with her teacher Linda for four years. Linda and I would go out to eat together—we had a lot in common and were the same age. But Kelly was at that in-between stage, between beginning and intermediate and I didn't think this teacher ever took her students past that stage. So we tried out a very professional man who cost us double the money. Lessons with him now are not warm and personal. They are just music, music, and straight to the point. But in the hour that he spends with Kelly, he gives her so much that it is well worth the price. He can look at her and help her make changes really quick. He knows what he's doing. But then I had to tell Linda. (Oh...for about three months Kelly was taking lessons with both teachers. I thought we'd keep taking lessons with her, maybe just on reed making). So I called Linda and told her and she was very upset with me. I wanted Kelly to continue going to Linda, but Linda refused. She was so hurt. It wasn't what I wanted, but I guess it had to happen. She said to me, "I think it would be best if you don't come back any more." I was devastated. We no longer have any relationship at all. It still hurts, just to think about it.

- **Teaching at Advanced Levels**

The close bonds developed by teacher and student in the middle school or high school years become something quite different in the college or conservatory where the purpose of training is usually to produce a professional.

The one-on-one relationship of private music teacher and student in music conservatories bears striking resemblance to the medieval system of apprenticeship. In the Middle Ages, skills were passed down from generation to generation, the father teaching his son the art of shoemaking or metalwork or blacksmithing, the monk training the novice, and the mother teaching her daughter the domestic arts.

Often children interested in a craft like making pottery would be sent to live with the potter, serving as his assistant while learning his trade. Both parties benefited from this arrangement which could last for years—the potter got free labor and the apprentice got room, board, and an education. When the boy had served his time as a lowly apprentice and when he had learned all that the master craftsman could teach him, he became "certified" to practice pottery on his own.

In today's music conservatories, music teachers are the masters of their trade, the skilled craftspeople possessing secret knowledge that they choose to pass on to the students worthy of receiving their gifts. Their students become their devoted protégés. Demanding auditions make sure that only those with the requisite skills can enter the hallowed gates of the conservatory.

The best of these teachers, in the best conservatories, are highly sought after, since their knowledge is required to prepare the young performer for the stage. Their influence is enormous. Unlike professors in the university system however, these private music teachers are rarely supervised by committees or evaluated for their pedagogical effectiveness. As a result, the actual quality of teaching varies enormously. Most of these teachers are truly excellent. A few cultivate their favorite student and disregard the others, condescend to teach, or don't show up for lessons. Some can spend much of the lesson recounting stories from their glory days.

Chapter Eight: Private Teachers

Conservatory teachers occupy a position not unlike a prophet or a priest. They have enormous power because only they have the secret skills and information needed by the young performer. Only they can pass on to the next generation the secrets of their trade. A student studies with the teacher for as many years as the conservatory teacher deems necessary. Only when the teacher pronounces the student "ready," is the student allowed to proceed. At that point, the prophetic mantle is passed on to a new disciple.

In concert program notes, an artist is described as being "the student of So-and-So." Often the names of several teachers will be given. This testifies to the legitimacy, the lineage, and the authority now vested in a new artist. There is a sense of royalty—a blood line of artists, each a descendent of the teachers who went before. This is how a new artist gains credibility and goes out into the world as a professional.

CHAPTER NINE

COST AND BENEFIT ANALYSIS FOR PARENTS

It is the rare school district that offers a comprehensive instrumental music program. As a result, those families that value music education usually undertake to finance it themselves. The cost of instruments and private lessons can add up. "Our budget is rent, food, and music," says the mother of two young musicians. Another laughs, "Braces and music lessons for three kids—you want to know why I'm broke?"

Despite the costs, families do succeed in giving their children music training. Many of these families are extremely creative. Here are some of the ways they manage.

- **How Children Help Out**

Most parents pay the music education bill, but many kids today help to defray the costs. Kids in middle and high school can certainly help to pay for their musical expenses. They save their birthday money, their Christmas presents, and their Bar Mitzvah checks. They work in the summer for banks, pharmacies, and caterers. They work as nurses' helpers, waiters, stock boys, grass cutters and leaf rakers. One girl went with her mother "to do house cleaning for some people." Another used old-fashioned bartering. Sharon cleaned her teacher's house, trading two hours of her cleaning time for one hour of her teacher's teaching time.

Living in rural Indiana, a clarinet player made his money delivering newspapers. Said his mother,

> For seven years he delivered newspapers, seven days a week. Classically American. He had his paper route and he did it every day after school. We are one of the few places in the country that still has kids doing delivery routes. If he did it on his bike, he could do it in half an hour. It only took ten minutes if I took him in the car. I kind of liked that, because then he would tell me about how his day went. On Sunday morning, my husband would take him on his route and afterwards, they would go have muffins. That's when *they* got to talk. He earned enough money to buy himself a much better clarinet.

There aren't too many children delivering newspapers any more. But there are still children who share and who know how to do without. The mother of two boys, one in first grade and one in fourth, faced a tight financial period. When she finally decided to get her son music lessons, she called a conference where the boys made this decision: they would take brown bag lunches to school instead of buying lunch, and would use their lunch money to help pay for private lessons. The amount they saved may not have been significant, but what they learned certainly was.

Learning to sacrifice today to get something you want tomorrow is a valuable lesson for all children. So is learning to find solutions to problems, working industriously, and saving what you earn. When Kate wanted to learn to play the harp, she found one that cost $500 for three months' rental. Her parents offered to pay for her lessons if she could earn the $500 for the first harp rental. Her mother said,

> Kate was racking her brains for a way to make the money when some men came by the neighborhood painting numbers on curbs and charging everyone $10. A light went off in Kate's head and she said, "I could do that and charge only $5!" She bought highway reflective paint, sprayed it on, and got up early every day to paint those numbers on the curbs. She worked that whole summer, explaining to the neighbors that she was trying to get a harp and how expensive it was. It took three months for her to earn the whole sum. In the meantime, as she approached her goal, we called this music place in Maryland (because you don't just go out and buy a harp). They ordered the harp and had it waiting for her. The very day that she got to the $500 mark, we drove to pick up her harp and she had her first lesson.

Many high-school kids make money by giving music lessons to younger children and a few are skilled enough to make money by actually performing on their instruments. In big cities with a street culture, kids can play on the street with their instrument case on the sidewalk and make more than a few bucks on a good night. In the trade, this is called "busking."

The mother of an accomplished harpist was pleased when her daughter earned enough to pay for her own sheet music, strings, and insurance by performing at weddings. Said the mother, "It was good business experience, but it wasn't problem-free. My big problem was living in dread that she would forget to show up at some poor bride's wedding." Parents never get off scot-free.

- **Scholarship Awards and Prize Money**

Many parents dream of scholarships, as do their children. The mother of three young musicians says,

> There's no way we could pay for all this ourselves. I sincerely believe that if we put out a solid effort, the doors that need to open will open. We're counting on scholarships—big, fat ones.

There *is* money available to talented students. Competitions award cash prizes, music camps offer tuition-free summer programs, and music schools give scholarships. Organizations like the Young Musicians Foundation support a whole roster of deserving young musicians by paying for years of lessons. A national symphony concerto competition can award $1,000 to the winner. A state competition can award $800. These prizes help defray, but seldom cover, the costs of music training.

- **Instruments on Loan**

When young musicians excel and receive recognition (usually in the form of winning competitions), they may get really lucky and be offered the loan of an instrument. Arts institutions or patrons of the arts may own valuable string instruments which they lend to the most promising young performers. In Los Angeles, a 14-year-old violinist started out playing a $500 instrument. Then the Colburn School of Music lent him a much more expensive instrument for several years. Later, a private donor gave him, on loan, a priceless Amati violin.

In Cleveland, Chicago, and in New Jersey, Soovin also acquired his instruments from generous benefactors, as his grateful father explains:

> At the Cleveland Institute of Music, my son's teacher found a member of the Cleveland Orchestra who let Soovin borrow his violin. My son played it for at least three years and the owner took care of the insurance—all Soovin had to do was to pay for regular maintenance services. He used this instrument for his Kennedy Center Debut recital and, a year later, he won the Paganini Violin Competition in Italy.
>
> Then the Strad Society of Chicago loaned him a violin and with it he won a Henryk Szeryng Foundation Audition in Monaco.
>
> At that time, a well-known violin collector in New Jersey offered Soovin the two-year loan of a Stradivarius and it was with that violin that he recorded his first CD.

Chapter Nine: Cost And Benefit Analysis For Parents

> Today, my son is playing on an instrument from the Strad Society in Chicago. His current loan is renewed every year and he is paying only for the insurance, and incidental costs.

The Chicago-based Stradivari Society was founded as a way to support young artists who are reaching for the pinnacle of their art, and who need a superb instrument in order to compete and reach their potential. These Italian violins with names like Amati, Stradivar, and Guarneri del Gesu are 18th-century masterpieces. Most experts agree that their rich sound has never been equaled by modern technology or craftsmanship; however, these violins, valued in the millions of dollars, are virtually unattainable by a young artist. Hence, the kind of modern-day patronage practiced by organizations such as the Strad Society.

- **Parental Sacrifices**

Most families, of course, will have no need for such extremely valuable instruments. But renting and purchasing a run-of-the-mill instrument can also be expensive. Some families have to take on debt. "We put the instruments on a charge card and were fortunate to be able to pay them off with my husband's annual bonus," reported the mother of two string players.

A New York family that refinanced their home, and Florida parents who took out a second mortgage, are not atypical. The Florida family asked their daughter to "sign a family contract saying that she had to take this seriously, since it was such a big commitment" for them. They told their daughter, "This is not your harp. This is our harp and it can be taken away." Meant as a serious statement of ownership rather than an empty threat, this agreement served as a powerful motivator for their appreciative daughter.

The single mother of a budding pianist sold a piece of family-owned real estate in order to purchase the grand piano her child's teacher said he needed. A California family liquidated a retirement account when they had to buy a piano, a string bass, and a bassoon for their children, all in the same year. A Pennsylvania mother dipped into her 401K, to buy a new cello. Having only a meager savings account, the father of two musicians took on a second job to finance music lessons. He spent a few 16-hour days working that year but, when he heard his children play, he felt that his effort had been well worth it.

Sacrifices were made by everyone in these families, but most were made willingly. As this Kentucky mother said, "It's not like we feel we're suffering. We feel blessed in another way. I guess we could take vacations—we used to take them—but we don't really miss them." Says the mother of a Michigan horn player, "For a number of years, 'vacation' has meant taking a child to music camp, or picking one up from camp. But we felt that this was a reasonable choice."

Mothers may choose not to wear the latest fashions as a way to manage their budget. Josh's mother says, "We have done our best to help our children pursue their dreams and I don't regret that. Sometimes I resent my ten-year-old wardrobe, though!" A family may choose not to frequent the finest restaurants. Ellen's mother says, "We may have eaten ground beef and noodles at home, but we focused our family life on being available to our children and giving them opportunities to pursue their dreams."

It often happens that families begin music lessons with a modest investment and then find, to their surprise, that improving skills incur higher costs. The stressed mother of three talented wind players explained,

> Once your kid is introduced to a higher level of musicianship, he doesn't want to go back to the low-level stuff. When that happens, you've got to keep paying for the high-level stuff. My kids keep flying ahead faster than I would have expected and I've got to keep on coming up with the money to pay for it. This is where it gets dicey.

Sacrificing for the children's happiness is not a modern phenomenon. Showing a German writer his old spinet, Guiseppe Verdi, the composer of such famous operas as *Aida* and *La Traviata*, said, "Yes, I did my first lessons on this old spinet, and for my parents it was a large sacrifice to get me this wreck, which was already old at that time; having it made me happier than a king." [53]

Why would any parent agree to spend such sums of money and time on music education?

Most parents want to educate their children, to expose them to the "finer things in life," to give them an artistically broadening experience. When their children show any degree of facility or talent, parents are justifiably proud of them. In addition, research now verifies the enormous benefits that children gain from music education. (Chapters Eleven and Twelve describe these benefits in greater detail.)

- **The Proud Parent Syndrome**

Parental pride is lampooned in an anecdote told about Shostakovich's mother. She brought her son to a piano teacher and announced: "I've brought you a marvelous pupil." To which the piano teacher responded: "All mothers have marvelous children." [54] Which, of course, is true.

When exaggerated, pride can lead to the kind of over-indulgence exhibited by the composer Bizet's mother who, according to legend, changed his shirt for him while he was practicing, so that he wouldn't need to take any time away from the piano.[55]

Some parents become "stage mothers," advocating fiercely for their children, pushing them far beyond their capabilities and well beyond what is seemly. One mother, bringing her high-school daughter to a well known conservatory for a piano audition, became distraught when her daughter failed to advance to the second round of auditions. She demanded to speak to the president of the conservatory, became violently hysterical, refused to leave the premises, and finally had to be removed by the local police.

Most proud parents, however, are more stable. The common problem they share is uncontrolled "bragging." If your son is out rehearsing for an orchestral performance and your friend's son is out doing drugs, you are wise not to mention your son's name any more than is necessary. That is basic to being considerate and kind in social situations. Because of this, some parents feel they must constantly watch what they say about their children. A proud Nebraska mother explained how she manages this:

> I am real careful when I talk to some folks, because I've been so lucky with my boy. I used to brag a lot, but now I don't want to say something that will offend, especially with the folks that are having trouble with their kids right now. You have to be careful how you talk or else people will get real upset with you. So when I am with the parents of other kids in the orchestra it feels real good, because I can tell it like it is. We understand each other.

Though they seldom admit it, proud parents do enjoy the opportunity for bragging that their musical children provide them.

- **Giving What You Didn't Get as a Child**

Many parents have a strong desire to give their children what they themselves wanted as children and feel they didn't get. If parents weren't given music lessons when they were young, they want to provide music lessons for their child, and they may use their own ambitions and frustrations to propel their children's progress. A successful violinist, who grew up in South Carolina with limited resources, expressed tremendous appreciation for the sacrifices her parents made to provide her with what they themselves had not received:

> The cost for my instrument, lessons, and travel gradually built up and put a huge strain on my parents. They sold their business and a condo, all because they felt that I truly would be the next…I don't know what…I'm grateful for all the sacrifices they made. That's why I am where I am today. But I do feel awful for them because they gave up so much for a gamble. You see, they had big dreams when they were younger, but never had the support from their parents, neither financial nor emotional. And they wanted me to realize my dream. They did everything in their power to help me achieve.

Chapter Nine: Cost And Benefit Analysis For Parents

This phenomenon is demonstrated by the immigrant mother of a talented violinist. Growing up in the countryside of Korea a quarter-century ago, this mother had never heard Western classical music. In her own words:

> We heard Korean music and folk songs when I was young, but not classical. When I went to college in Seoul, the big city, it was culture shock. I met for the first time people who had had piano lessons when they were young. Classical music it's a kind of showing what class you are—that was our culture in Korea in 1972. If you are a college student, you have to know about music but, if you're like me, never exposed, you go to sneak around and get some tapes and try to listen at home so when you go to concerts you can remember the rhythms and sounds. Maybe that's why today we want to be involved with the music. When I finish college, I always have in my mind, you know, one day you marry and have children. I wanted them exposed to culture. I had such a big lack in my life personally. And when baby came along—I'm going to have music and art! I take my baby to all the children's concerts.

- **How Parents Benefit from Their Children's Music Education**

Other parents have benefited socially from their children's involvement with music. As a result of spending time at rehearsals and other musical activities, they have met interesting adults from diverse backgrounds and have made lasting friends. As chaperones for youth orchestras, they have exhilarating experiences, traveling to concerts in Europe, Asia, and Australia.

Listening to a child perform can be a "deep emotional experience" for a parent. One mother said:

> When my daughter goes to the piano in the living room and starts to play the Saenz-Saints Second Piano Concerto, I have to hold back the tears, she is so wonderful and the music is so beautiful.

A Texas mother tells this story,

> The first time we walked into City Hall, I looked around and thought, "My 14-year old is going to play on this stage?" I stood stock still, teared up, and felt transported to a higher plane. Just thinking about it now brings tears to my eyes.

Or, in the words of this mother,

> For Mother's Day, Neal played Ave Maria from the choir loft. I couldn't imagine a nicer Mother's Day gift. It was gorgeous, absolutely gorgeous, it echoed through the church, and I was reduced to...nothing. I was just bawling.

This kind of reaction has a religious quality, as conveyed by this devout mother:

> I believe music is a gift from God. The ability to play and the purpose of music is divine, if used correctly. That's what music is for, I think. What did Bach say? The purpose of music is to draw you closer to God? But Bach said it more eloquently. I'll have to look up that quotation. When Glenda plays beautifully, it draws me closer to the Lord. My hope for her is that she will use her musical talent to draw herself and her audience closer to our Heavenly Father, because there is no higher purpose.

Another emotional (and social) reward parents experience is the sense of giving to the community. Performing music at charity events, nursing homes, and hospitals gives parents and children spiritual satisfaction. "It's a real win-win-win situation," said a mother from Georgia. "The audience gets entertained, the kids get performance opportunities, and we parents rejoice in the whole endeavor."

- **Costs and Benefits for Family Life**

Family life can be significantly enhanced by sharing, performing, and enjoying music together. Only 50 years ago, it was not unusual for families to gather around the upright piano to play and sing together, in a scene familiar to us from Norman Rockwell paintings. Today that is a rare scene.

Chapter Nine: Cost And Benefit Analysis For Parents

When one child in a family performs, whether on the soccer field, in the school play, glee club, or youth concert, the whole family can enjoy attending the event and supporting the performer. When a brother is performing in concert, his siblings can derive pleasure from seeing him on stage, and can share in his moment of attention and glory.

For many siblings, however, these performances can also result in stress, unhappy competition, and simple jealousy. An older brother may resent his parents' assumptions that he will attend his younger brother's performance. Even when it's not a matter of jealousy, older brothers simply have better things to do with their time.

- **Competition Between Siblings**

Competition, when it's not excessive, has a healthy role in society. As adults we all compete for honor and success in our various venues, and our children compete in school and on the playground—good competition is the basis of most good games. At home, children compete as well, for space, power, "goodies," and for parental attention and affection.

When one child plays an instrument and receives considerable attention, it may spur siblings to follow in his or her footsteps and to take up an instrument of their own. When this happens, it is preferable to have siblings play different instruments so as to minimize unhappy comparisons. Siblings compare themselves anyway. When a younger sister compares herself to her older sibling, she usually loses out. It doesn't help much to tell a child that music is undertaken for the sake of enjoyment, not competition. Explaining that a child should be more patient, that improvement will come as he or she grows, has little impact. Children don't usually have that much patience.

What can be worse, however, is when a younger child outshines her older brother or sister. This is not at all uncommon and is often a reason that older siblings stop playing an instrument. Parents with two or three children who all study music sometimes report that they first realized the exceptional talent of their younger child when he or she outperformed older siblings.

If siblings play different instruments, it avoids the worst of the competition and can result in shared music-making, especially if the two instruments are compatible for chamber music groupings. One mother found that when her two sons played different instruments (flute and trumpet) it helped minimize their competition. She tells this story:

> One day Jarrod told Neal, "That sounds terrible. You're not playing very good on that flute." So Neal handed him the flute and said, "Go ahead, I dare you." I swear, Jarrod couldn't get a note out of that flute to save his life. They are utterly unable to play each other's instruments, so that keeps the competition under control.

Siblings on different instruments are more ready to encourage one another, laugh off setbacks, and share each other's successes. They are more interested in attending one another's recitals and performances, and they are generally more understanding and forgiving. Brothers and sisters who play instruments may have greater sympathy for their sibling's needs, and so their rapport and compatibility increase. A Florida family with a violinist and cellist reports that "everyone goes to everyone's concerts unless they really cannot. The concerts are on the family calendar and are just a part of life. The kids know that they have to support each other, and they do.

- **Guilt, Resentment, and the "Other" Child**

Siblings of musicians, especially younger ones, may have to endure certain unpleasant activities like being dragged along in the car to music lessons and rehearsals. Most parents dislike inconveniencing one sibling for the sake of another, and sometimes the parents feel guilty.

When a child says from an early age that he or she wants to be a musician, his older siblings—who have no professional ambitions—can think something is "wrong" with them for not having a clear

Chapter Nine: Cost And Benefit Analysis For Parents

direction of their own. They have to be reassured that most children their age have no idea of what they want to do when they grow up.

As a result, some parents try to "make it up" to the child who is not interested in music. A Pennsylvania mother worries, "Sometimes I feel bad for my daughter. She tries so much harder than Trevor, but she never seems to do quite as well. When she does accomplish something, she is thrilled and so we have to make a bigger deal out of it than we really should." This is true in any family, of course, when one child is more successful than another. But, with the exception of athletics and other performing arts such as theater and dance, successes in most activities (including academics) are not as dramatically public as are those in music. Music is performed on stage with the audience quietly attentive and the performance is followed by applause. When a brother excels academically, however, his sister does not have her brother's talent and success paraded in front of her, nor is she consigned to applaud him from her seat in the audience.

Because a parent has to frequently drive a child to musical activities, and often must stay for lessons or rehearsals, the left-out child can feel the parent spends more time with the sister or brother. Parents suffer when their "other" child says, "You love him more than me."

Because the pursuit of music can be costly, the "other" children may feel slighted. The brother of Leopold Stokowski, the great conductor of the Philadelphia Orchestra, experienced this. Remembering his childhood, he said, "My father did everything for Leo and spent what little money he had on his music. I am afraid my sister Lydia had I had to suffer, as there was nothing left for us." [56]

When families have more than one musical child, auditioning can mean double trouble. One family living near Chicago brought their two children to audition for the Metropolitan Youth Symphony Orchestra. Their son, a trombonist, wanted desperately to play in this orchestra. Their younger daughter came along for the ride and decided to audition just for the experience and the "fun" of it.

You guessed it. The boy didn't get into the orchestra, but his younger sister did. His mother later learned that her son didn't make it because the orchestra didn't need a trombone. What they needed was a *bass* trombone. She immediately called her son and said, "Thomas, quick! Find a bass trombone—you've got two weeks until the auditions to learn how to play it!" Thomas' high school happened to have a bass trombone. He took it home, practiced like crazy, and actually won his audition, winning a place in the orchestra along with his sister. But most auditioning stories don't end so neatly.

- **Benefits for Families**

In spite of these sibling issues, parents generally feel that music has significantly strengthened their families. As much as they complain about the time that music takes (particularly the driving time), parents overwhelmingly feel that the time spent on music served to cement family bonds. As one Orange County mother put it,

> The drive time to and from lessons and rehearsals gave me one-on-one time with my teen-agers that I dare say most parents do not enjoy with their kids. I wouldn't trade those hour-plus trips to and from LA for anything in the world.

Going to lessons, rehearsals, performances, parades, recitals, and competitions means time spent together. Not everyone would consider this quality time. But if used for talking, that is what it can become.

Many families believe that the difficulties and sacrifices they shared to make music training possible brought them closer together. The violinist from South Carolina recalls:

> Every weekend my dad and I had to come to Philadelphia. Actually, we drove to Philly more than twice a week for my lessons. During one winter the heater in the car broke down and we couldn't afford to fix it, so we took thick blankets with us all winter long. That went on for a couple of years. So you see, for the sake of my musical education, my parents really had to do without a lot. But here's the wonderful thing: Because of those times when there was such a financial struggle, our

Chapter Nine: Cost And Benefit Analysis For Parents

family grew closer together and learned to depend and lean on each other. I wouldn't trade that for anything in the world.

For some children, a parent who knows little about music serves as the perfect, all-accepting audience. A Tennessee mother whose husband is in the trucking industry says,

> Every evening when my husband comes home he says to our son, "Rob, come and play for me." Since he doesn't have a critical ear, Rob loves to play for him best of all. It sounds funny, but the two of them have really bonded this way.

In other families where the parents are musical, their children's music gives them a lot to talk about, as this Nebraska mother explains:

> My husband and son both play the trumpet, and they have so much to say to each other. Sharing of equipment over the years has created a strong bond between them. There were these special trumpets that Brian couldn't use until "some day" when his father decided he was worthy of them. And when the day finally came, it was a real milestone for him! The two of them have become very close because their lives have intertwined and influenced each other. It's real good to see how their common interest connected them.

That kind of experience can be especially meaningful when it involves multiple generations. A father talks about seeing his own father watch his granddaughter's performance:

> My father is a hard-bitten ex-Marine, not given to emotion. He was a clarinetist in his youth though, and both of his parents had been musical. When he came to visit and heard my daughter Evie in her flute ensemble, I could pretty much read his thoughts. There I was, watching him see his mother and father on one end and Evie on the other, and reveling in the continuity and family connection. He had tears in his eyes, something I have only seen twice in the 50 years I have known him.

- **Educational Benefits for Parents**

Non-musical parents of musical children almost universally recount the pleasure they have experienced learning about classical music because their children are studying it. This father in Atlanta, Georgia, is typical:

> This wonderful thing has just taken us completely by surprise. It's not something we were prepared for at all. We are from the Beatles generation, not much into classical music. For us, a violin was a fiddle, everything you blew into was a horn, and whatever you beat on was a drum. But now we're starting to love listening to classical stuff. It just trickled down from our daughter to the rest of the family. We started buying a lot of CD's. If we're in the car listening to the radio, we can say, "Oh, that's an oboe or a clarinet or a flute. It's been an education for us and also for my siblings who were never exposed to classical music. Now they see it as something *they* want for *their* children. It's been a great gift.

A San Francisco mother learned the most about music simply by attending her daughter's rehearsals:

> When the conductor rehearses the youth orchestra, I listen. Others take books or knitting, but I listen and learn. I can sit there and hear what he tells them and then, when they do it, I can hear it. Then I understand what the conductor meant. I see from one week to the next the improvement. I say, "Oh, yes, that's it." I get it. Ever since I started listening to their rehearsals, I started understanding, a bit, the music, and what the musicians are trying to do.

Another woman said,

> I'm getting so much out of my kids' music, it's unbelievable. I sit in on their lessons, and I sit in on the wind ensemble rehearsals. I sit in as much as they'll let me sit in because I found out that I've got a certain hunger now to understand what they're doing. It's starting to make sense to me in ways that it didn't before. I understand now how to figure out which key the piece is in, you know "fat cats go down alleys eating barks." I know now how to count 7/8 time—that's my new thing. It's starting to not seem as hard as it did before.

Or, as one mother expressed:

> The best thing about our son's music is what it's done for my husband who's a real Texas redneck. Now he says, "I'm really beginning to like this Beethoven dude."

- **Parental Stress**

When children compete, they may sweat and tremble nervously, or they may act cool and collected, but most parents admit that they themselves are always anxious at their children's competitions. The mother of a pianist said,

> I was always nervous for Kira when she went to competitions. When your child is used to success, the one thing you fear is a serious failure, one that might be disabling for them. You just don't know how they're going to take failure when they've gotten used to success.

The father of a French horn player agreed, adding that the reason he gets nervous at performances is that he knows "it only takes a second, and something goes wrong that, you know, you can't fix on stage. That's enough to make anyone nervous."

The mother of a pianist was concerned about how a defeat would affect her son, until he turned to her and said, "Mom, there are going to be 25 kids competing for one prize and if I don't win this time, maybe I'll win next time. So stop worrying!" From that point on, she tried to relax.

The mother of a successful oboist learned from her son's teacher not to "agonize." Whenever the mother became upset about a competition, she would repeat the teacher's mantra: "We don't agonize about these things." The mother learned to stay as calm as her son needed her to be. "Aaron had his share of disappointments, but he never let them stop him," she said. "He just picked himself up and went on, murmuring, 'We don't agonize.'"

The mother of a trumpet player describes her state of mind at her son's last audition:

> When he went for the Southern California State Band and Orchestra Association audition, I was an absolute nervous wreck. For sure I was more nervous than he was. I was sweating from head to toe. I was breathing for him. I could hear him in the audition room because I was in the outer area waiting for him and I knew where he had to take a big breath, so I was taking it for him. Only a mother!

- **Parental Growth**

Some parents decide that they need to do more than appreciate—they want to *participate* in music. This Pittsburgh mother said, "One of these days, after Cecile leaves home, I'll have time to take lessons myself!" Or in the words of the oboist's mother, "Aaron may have left home, but he has filled our life with music. I do my own music, singing in a choir, attending concerts, and now I'm also playing the cello!"

These New York parents speak with sophistication about how their personal growth stemmed from their son's music:

> Our son has exposed us to so many facets of life that we would never have experienced on our own. He opened our eyes and ears to the different rhythmic patterns in life. He forced us to find congruity and consonance in a most seemingly dissonant aural experience. By extension, we have been able to "read" a sense of order in the most chaotic of life's experiences.

Music education, though high in cost, is also high in reward. Many parents assert that, for themselves and for their children, learning to play music pays far greater dividends than simply hearing music sweetly played. The gift of music that parents give their children is also a gift these parents give to their families and to themselves, a gift that brings to all of them social, emotional, psychological and personal growth.

CHAPTER TEN

GOING PRO

Towards the end of their high school years, students who are skilled musicians and love performing will have to decide whether to pursue music as a profession. Their parents have to decide whether and how to support them in their decision making.

- **Competitions**

Auditions and competitions are an unavoidable part of this decision-making process. Many people, musicians included, say that music should not be about competing—it should be about cooperating. As one young violinist said,

> It's not right to do competitions in music, because music is too open. It's not like track where the person who runs fastest wins. Music isn't a race. It's more like writing essays. Everyone has a story to tell and everyone's story is worth

hearing. I hate competitions! I prefer playing chamber music because then I am cooperating, not competing.

But most competitions are taken in stride and some students even enjoy them. One girl who auditioned on bass for a student orchestra didn't "make it," but felt the audition was a "wonderful experience" and that she had learned from it. The judges for these competitions often take notes on student performances and then share these notes with the student, giving them valuable feedback.

My son received unanticipated feedback after his first audition for a Young Musicians Foundation scholarship. Jonathan had rushed straight from school to the audition site, wearing his standard torn jeans. He arrived to find the other boys, more experienced in auditioning, wearing suits; the little girls wore pink taffeta. After Jonathan's performance, the judge wrote several helpful comments about technical aspects of his playing and then dryly added: "May I suggest that for your next audition a less informal attire may be more appropriate for the occasion."

Winning a competition, naturally, can be exhilarating and it can be a crucial factor in a student's decision making. The mother of a cellist feels that her daughter's success in one competition helped the girl gauge her ability, and it encouraged her to study music at the college level. Although it is important to have confidence in your own ability without needing validation from others, well-run competitions do provide some objective indication of talent. This is important input for students deciding on a career path.

Some students really "go after" competitions, applying for everything that comes their way, making calls, sending off tapes, and traveling to competitions wherever they are held. These students enjoy the adrenaline rush and revel in the excitement that competing provides. Others are lured into competitions by the offers of scholarships with cash prizes to help offset the costs of buying and maintaining an instrument.

- **College Auditioning**

High-school students who have decided to study music seriously have two choices: they can apply to a liberal arts college where they major in music, or to a conservatory which is a high-pressure vocational school for musicians. In either case, they will need to audition as part of the application process. They may travel to the school for the audition, or the school may hold regional try-outs. The most competitive schools, like the more highly rated teachers, will require that students travel to them.

It shocked me as a parent to learn that the audition determining my son's fate would take no more than 10 or 15 minutes. The only thing that mattered would be this brief audition. Forget his academic record. Ignore his swim team medals. Don't bother with personal recommendations from teachers. SAT scores? Irrelevant. None of that other stuff counted. The only thing of importance was how Jonathan sounded on his flute for 15 minutes on that one day.

"But what if he has a bad day?" I protested. That would simply be too bad. "What if he's sick that day?" It would be a shame. "What if he arrives late to the audition?" (A real possibility for my son.) That would be an automatic strike-out. There would be no second chances. Of course, Jonathan would be welcome to audition the following year, but for now, that would be it.

A young musician has been practicing, perhaps several hours a day, for years, and it comes down to this single, tense 15-minute snippet of playing.

Who makes the decision to accept or reject a student candidate? You might think it would be a committee decision, and sometimes it is. There may be three or four staff musicians who listen to the auditions. But often it is only one person who hears the student and makes the admissions decision. This means that those decisions can be highly personal and idiosyncratic. Of course there is always a certain degree of subjectivity in judging a musical performance. But the truth is that good musicianship is abundantly evident to those who understand it. Very seldom will two professional teachers disagree substantially about the quality of a student performance. They may differ in their appreciation of a student's musical interpretation, but not in their evaluation of a student's technical ability or promise as a performer.

Auditions can have unexpected twists. Most music majors recall at least one near miss in their short careers. One of the worst is illness, which can obliterate years of work, as this mother of an Oberlin violinist recalls:

> On the morning of her Oberlin audition, Marlin awoke with a temperature of 102 degrees! She felt terrible, but she had no choice—they don't do make-ups. All those years of hard work and it came down to a 15-minute audition! She was really sick. So I gave her two Tylenols and she played. She was on fire, but she played.

Not all auditions are fair. Sometimes judges face what can most charitably be called "conflicts of interest." Especially at conservatories, but also in university music departments, the instrumental teachers judge which students are accepted. These teachers may also give lessons to talented younger students who later apply for admission and, in such cases, conflicts can occur. To explain this in the most generous terms, a teacher may accept into the conservatory a student he is already teaching, simply because the teacher knows how well that student plays. The teacher has only a short audition with other students in which to gauge their abilities. This is not uncommon, although it may seem terribly unfair. Most, but not all, judges will step aside in such a situation, but that decision is usually left to the judge's discretion.

A West Coast mother brought her daughter to audition at a fine Midwestern conservatory and was shocked to learn how other students had curried favor with the prestigious Russian violin teacher who taught there:

> One girl came to the audition with a bouquet of flowers for the judge! She already knew the judge because she was her

teacher! Once a week she had flown to the school for a lesson with this teacher! Of course, she had a huge advantage over my daughter and the other newcomers. Flowers! You know that this is not a blind, fair audition! I felt like such a dumb mother—I didn't know that this kind of thing went on!

- **A Child's Certainty**

When my son Jonathan was nine, he announced that he was going to become the principal flutist of a major American orchestra. He insisted, all the way through high school, that what he wanted to do was play flute—no, play *first* flute—in a major orchestra. Because he would be a flutist, he told us, he would have no need to learn to write good English or to study world history. In fact, he said, he wouldn't need a high school diploma at all. His utter certainty and stubbornness exasperated us.

Thick-skulled determination is not uncommon among children who decide that they want to become professional musicians. When she was in sixth grade, a Michigan horn player announced that she wanted to play in a symphony orchestra. To this day, says her bewildered mother, "She has never wavered or changed her mind."

As an adult, it is unnerving to face a child's certainty when you see only possibility—and a limited possibility, at that. You can respond with anger and frustration, or you can tolerate what the child is saying with a degree of respect. It can feel as if the child is responding to a force beyond himself and it feels scary. This kind of fearfulness is akin to awe.

Samuel Barber was so sure he would become a composer, that he wrote his mother this letter at the age of nine:

NOTICE to *Mother* and *nobody else*

Dear Mother: I have written this to tell you my worrying secret. Now don't cry when you read it because it is neither yours nor my fault. I suppose I will have to tell it now without any nonsense. To begin with I was not meant to be an athlet (sic). I was meant to be a composer, and will be I'm sure. I'll

> ask you one more thing.—Don't ask me to try to forget this unpleasant thing and go play football.—Please—Sometimes I've been worrying about this so much that it makes me mad (not very).
>
> Love,
>
> Sam Barber II [57]

Unfortunately, we have no record of Mrs. Barber's response. Upon hearing such a declaration, many parents today might smile and wait for this phase to pass. When it doesn't pass, however, parents may come to accept and even to support their child's dream. Parents today want their children to do what they love to do. The mother of an Arizona college wind player figured that if her musical son "does what he loves, it will all work out. If he doesn't get a position this year, he will go on to graduate school and then get an agent. He'll find a way."

The American composer, Ned Rorem, tells this story about how his father was won over to the idea that his son would become a composer.

> "How do you plan to make a living?" asked Father, on learning that I wanted to be a composer when I grew up. Apparently I replied, "What difference does it make, if I can't be a composer?" That answer was so un-American as to impress Father, who, although a breadwinner, took seriously his not-so-sublimated baritone. To his eternal credit he agreed then and there to be supportive of the family freak.[58]

- **Parental Opposition**

Parents who discourage their children's musical ambitions are legendary. Many famous musicians battled parents who were firmly opposed to their musical aspirations.

Beethoven's childhood friend recalled that Beethoven's father was often critical of his son's improvised melodies on the violin. The friend remembered this incident:

Chapter Ten: Going Pro

> Once he was playing without notes; his father happened in and said: What silly trash are you scraping away at now? You know that I can't bear that; scrape according to the notes; otherwise your scraping won't be of much use." [59]

It would be interesting to know how that cranky father would have felt after hearing his son's famous fifth symphony, but he died before it was written.

In our own century, the flutist Jean-Pierre Rampal faced a father who was a professional flutist and teacher. Rampal remembers wanting to emulate his father, but he experienced a harsh response:

> When I was about six, I came across an old wooden flute, which thrilled me no end. It was a soprano flute, the kind used to fake an instrument in theatrical productions. I could put this instrument to my lips, blow and sound just like my father—well, not exactly like him. The noise from my little wooden flute had none of the tone, sonority or grace that emanated from my father's silver flute.
>
> "Stop that terrible screeching," said my father, putting his hands to his ears. "You can't play that instrument. It has a false sound."
>
> "But I want to play music."
>
> "That is not music." And he took the flute away from me. We had a furnace in our living room that was used to warm the house; he threw the pipe into the flames...This early failure did not alter my desire to play music.[60]

Only when Jean-Pierre was 12 did his father relent and allow him to start learning to play the flute.

The father of George Frederick Handel intended that his son study civil law and did everything possible to oppose his interest in music. The elder Doctor Handel forbad his son to play any instrument and removed all instruments from the house. He complained to his friends about his son's "uncontrollable humour," [61] but his friends and colleagues were not convinced the father would succeed.

> It was observed with reason, that where Nature seemed to declare herself in so strong a manner, resistance was often not only fruitless, but pernicious. Some said, that, from all the accounts, the case appeared so desperate, that nothing but the cutting off his fingers could prevent his playing; and others affirmed, that it was a pity any thing *should* prevent it. Such were the sentiments and declarations of the Doctor's friends in regard to his son.[62]

When the Duke of Saxe-Weisenfels heard Handel perform brilliantly at the organ, he tried to reason with Handel's father. Handel's father stood firm, however flattered he may have been by the attention of the "Prince":

> He [the father] was sensible of the Prince's goodness in taking such notice of his son, and giving his opinion concerning the best methods for his education. But he begged leave humbly to represent to his Highness, that though Music was an elegant art, and a fine amusement, yet if considered as an occupation, it had little dignity, as having for its object nothing better than mere pleasure and entertainment: that whatever degree of eminence his son might arrive at in such a profession, he thought that a much less degree in many others would be far preferable.[63]

The father of Hector Berlioz also refused to allow his son piano lessons. He wanted his son to pursue medicine, and he offered him this bribe: he would buy young Hector a new flute to play for fun if he promised to study medicine seriously.[64]

One father opposed to a musical life for his son tried compromising. He wanted his son to go to law school. He said, "I was not enamored with the idea of my son being a musician. When he finished high school, we agreed on a compromise—instead of law or music, he would study business." The son did study business in college, but he went on to become a successful baritone singing on the opera stage.

In the 20th century, the father most implacable to his child's musical ambition may have been Samuel Bernstein, the father of Leonard

Bernstein. Samuel was an intellectual in love with Jewish learning who had wanted to become a rabbi. Instead, he had gone into the beauty supply business in Boston running the Samuel Bernstein Hair Company. When his son's musical ambitions surfaced, Samuel could only think of the *klezmorim*, the impoverished, Jewish musicians of Eastern Europe who went like troubadours from town to town playing at weddings. There was no way he wanted that for his son. He refused to give Lenny private lessons and did everything possible to discourage the boy from studying music. When 12-year old Bernstein began studying piano with a teacher at the New England Conservatory of Music and had to come up with three dollars for his lessons, Samuel relented somewhat, but Lenny still had to pay for his lessons out of his weekly allowance.[65]

Years later, when Leonard Bernstein became a household name, his father Samuel was asked about his early opposition to his son's musical ambitions. In typical Jewish fashion, he answered the question with a question: "How did I know he was going to become Leonard Bernstein?" Later, in a more reflective mood, he mused, "You know, every genius had a handicap. Beethoven was deaf. Chopin had tuberculosis. Well, someday I suppose the books will say, 'Lenny Bernstein had a father.'" [66]

- **Parental Concern about Money**

The fact is that most people who pursue a career in music realize only modest financial rewards. Aware of this reality, parents whose children declare their desire to become professional musicians are concerned that they may wind up on the streets with hat in hand.

The father of a violinist whose son had already demonstrated his potential by winning a national competition and performing at Carnegie Hall said, "I just want to make sure my son can make a living, buy a house and a car, and have a normal life." The mother of a violinist studying at Oberlin School of Music said what many parents feel: "To have your child work so hard for so many years and get to be so good and then have only a small chance to be able to make any money at it is heartbreaking."

For some, the stakes are so high, the path so dim, and the prospects so murky that the decision to pursue music becomes a spiritual dilemma. The mother of a California pianist turned to prayer:

> I did a Novena, a nine-day prayer, to help her decide. I did a rosary every day and prayed for the same thing for nine consecutive days. Then the decision was clear: she will go on in music. She worried about how she would make living, since there's hardly an audience any more for classical music. But I told her: "I will be your sponsor. Mozart had a sponsor. I'll be yours." After my prayer, I was sure that she could do it if she wanted to. The next time she needed to make a decision, I didn't do just a Novena--I did a whole 40 days of Lent prayer.

This father of another musician wanted his son to go into law, but relented when he felt his son could "make it" financially:

> Unless you are the number one musician, you don't make very good money. I had tried to make money in music myself, but I only made a few hundred dollars and could not support my family on that. So, based on my experience, I wasn't at all enthusiastic about my son going into music. But when we understood what it meant to him and saw that he really could support himself, we were behind him. Today, he is singing at the opera in Paris. When the phone rings from Paris now, it is not a call for financial help.

The financial rewards of an orchestral musical career can vary enormously. Free-lance musicians struggle for gigs unless they play for a professional studio and these studios are located primarily in New York City and Los Angeles. In 2000-2001, musicians in the top orchestras in the United States (the New York Philharmonic, the Chicago Symphony, the Philadelphia Orchestra, the Cleveland Orchestra, and the Boston Symphony) had a minimum yearly salary of approximately $100,000, and the principal performers in these orchestras earned considerably more. Principal wind and string players may command even heftier sums in contract negotiations, with oboists, bassoonists, and French horn players pulling down the highest salaries. In one major American symphony, the concertmaster earned a salary of $367,000 for the 2003-2004 season. The same musician in a community orchestra, however, may be paid a salary as low as $24,000.

- **Parental Concern about Life Style**

In addition to money worries, parents also fret about what kind of life their child will live as a professional musician. "Will she lead a normal life or will she always be flying from one city to another?" "Will he be able to take the rejections and losses?" "Will she be able to have a family if she is always traveling?" "What kind of family life will he have if he is performing every night?" "Will my child be able to deal with the disappointment of *not* "making it" in the world of music?

All parents worry. But the parents of musicians stew about their child having too little in terms of possessions and recognition, and also about their having too much. Some parents worry about the heady life of excess enjoyed by well-known musicians. As one father put it:

> I feared my son might become too cozy with the rich life style of wealthy art patrons and highly privileged classical music lovers. When I heard that he had been driven by a charming female driver in a white limo from the Phoenix airport to a multi-room resort complex, I grimaced. Then there was a well-known oil company executive who took my son for a ride in his own hot-air balloon, a Central American business tycoon who had a maid specializing in ice-cream making, and European royalty in full regalia.

- **Accepting a Child's Musical Ambition**

Many parents who initially objected to their children's serious pursuit of music changed their attitude when independent outsiders validated their children's talent. One tuba player's parents insisted that he apply to liberal arts institutions when it was time for him to apply to college. They also allowed their son to apply to one top-notch conservatory. They figured that, if he got into the best music school, he was destined to be a performer. When their son was accepted by the conservatory, his parents accepted his path.

The Pleasures and Perils of Raising Young Musicians

The father of an accomplished violinist explains how he came to terms with his son's ambitions:

> Although I watched my son's commitment in high school to violin lessons, practicing, weekly rehearsals, auditions, competitions, and summer music camps, and although I generally supported his musical activities, I never believed that he would do music professionally. I always thought he could easily change gears to prepare himself for a career in any non-musical field. In fact, that was exactly what I was expecting him to do.
>
> When he began to discuss the idea of leaving home for a music school during his junior year, I was indescribably conflicted. We discussed his options for weeks. Finally, my wife and I struck a deal with him: he would test out his music-career option for the next four years and then re-evaluate the situation. Part of the bargain was that he would taste a liberal dose of philosophy, foreign language, English literature, history, and other traditional liberal arts subjects.
>
> But what happened is that once he was immersed almost full-time in music, this bargain became meaningless, because he never looked back. His enthusiasm for music and his sense of fulfillment made my commitment come more easily. Besides, there were many indicators of his promise as a performer and these provided strong reassurance of the validity of his judgment.

The father of the baritone who resolved the conflict of law versus music by urging his son toward a compromise in business explains how he finally accepted his son's choice:

> Nigel had been studying business in Montreal for two years. One winter break, we went to pick him up and bring him home. In the car, he handed a cassette to us and said, "Here, play this for me." So we stuck it into the car's cassette player and this fantastic voice came out singing in Russian. My immediate reaction: "Why, that sounds like Dietrich Fischer-Diskau. It's great. Who is that?"
>
> He said, "That's me." And it just blew us away. He had made such vast progress since we had heard him sing in high school!

And he was supposedly studying business! So from that point on, we took him seriously and we agreed to support his studying music. I had always known that he was *interested* in music, but that was the first time I realized he was talented.

- **Accepting Different Decisions**

Some parents are reluctant to accept their children's decisions to become professional musicians. Others are hard pressed to accept their children's decisions to give music up. Letting go of hopes and expectations for a child is perhaps the most difficult element of parenting. Over time, some children lose interest in music, while others find a new and more compelling interest. Some students get worn down by the demands of the professional music world and choose a different path— one they feel will bring them greater life satisfaction. After investing so much time, money, and energy in a child's musical education, parents can experience a sense of waste when it is abandoned.

It may help a parent in this situation to remember that their children learned much more than how to play notes, and that the deeper lessons taught by the study of music will sustain their children as they go on in life. Whatever your child does or does not do with his musical education is in some ways irrelevant. What is crucial is what the child has learned and will always possess. Children who have studied classical music will know how to set goals and work towards them, how to delay immediate gratification, how to pursue excellence and beauty, and how to work sensitively with others. We will look at these and other benefits of music study in the next two chapters.

CHAPTER ELEVEN

ACADEMIC AND INTELLECTUAL BENEFITS OF MUSIC STUDY

The connections between music study and academic achievement are not obvious, but they are real. Music teaches children to follow directions, accept instruction, cultivate academic discipline, commit to success, and concentrate on excellence. It teaches craftsmanship, high standards, goal setting, and the skill of measuring one's own progress. In addition, new research suggests that cognitive skills essential for mathematical and verbal reasoning are strengthened by the study of music.

Previous chapters have discussed how to support your child's music education—selecting an instrument, finding a teacher, and maintaining a practice schedule. Chapters 11 and 12 highlight the enormous benefits that music study offers children. When you are "tearing your hair out" over some aspect of this process, review these chapters to give yourself some needed support and encouragement.

- **Following Directions**

A large number of parents claim that when their children started studying music, their school work seemed to become easier and their grades actually improved. One clear reason for this is that playing an instrument required these children to learn the critical skill of following directions.

Teachers in today's schools spend an inordinate amount of time trying to teach children to follow directions. This skill may seem so elementary that it needn't be taught, but it is an ability that too few elementary-school children today have mastered. Today's children are frequently praised for their creativity and uniqueness, but rarely for their ability to simply do what they are told. Following directions has become politically incorrect; it is no longer deemed an important skill, but rather an unwelcome sign of submission to authority.

However, following a teacher's directions instead of one's own personal preferences is a crucial skill for learning. Anyone who has learned to fly an airplane, operate a forklift, or manage a switchboard must be able to follow directions. This skill is well taught by athletic coaches and by music teachers because trying to understand directions and following them as precisely as possible is what will determine athletic and musical success. Children who can accept instruction and follow directions so as to produce a clear note on the clarinet will then be able to follow the directions of teachers and experts in other fields as well.

Of course, following directions is not the only skill involved in academic success. Creativity is also important and is strongly valued and emphasized by today's parents and teachers. American children excel in creative endeavors. It is the balance of tight discipline and free creativity, however, that offers the best results in all fields—music, art, athletics, academics, and in life. For us to better achieve that balance, we need to place greater emphasis on the skill of following directions.

- **Discipline**

In addition to learning to follow directions, music students learn discipline. The skills learned through a disciplined study of music transfer to strong study skills, fluent communication skills, and enhanced cognitive abilities, all of which contribute to greater success in school.

When her son, a clarinetist, applied to medical school, a Michigan mother learned that the university admissions committee had been impressed by her son's commitment to music and by the discipline that his musical achievements demonstrated. In fact, one doctor surveyed medical school applicants and their undergraduate fields of concentration and found that the acceptance rate for music students applying to medical school was higher than that of students in any other undergraduate major, including the sciences! A whopping 66% of music majors who applied to medical school were admitted! By comparison, only 44% of biochemistry majors were accepted.[67]

It is a stretch to say that the best preparation for medical school is playing the violin, but there is a connection. Medical school admissions staffs recognize that serious music students have developed the commitment and discipline that they will need to succeed in the difficult field of medicine.

Parents, grateful for the academic boost they feel music has given their children, often speak of their children's improved self-discipline, concentration, and ability to focus. The mother of a student bass player explains what music has given her daughter:

> Eleanor didn't used to be a good student. But as she grew and developed into adulthood with her bass, she developed a whole lot of good things. Now this was a child who wouldn't carry a book much less read one. But as a senior she has done phenomenally well, especially in English, where she read lots and lots of books and enjoyed them, too. It's all the discipline

of the bass. Music requires making a commitment and, above all else, developing a personal sense of discipline.

Making music is a craft, and studying music teaches craftsmanship. Music students, needing to distinguish between the mediocre and the good, learn to identify excellence and strive to achieve it. After a time, students come to internalize basic standards of excellence. Music provides objective standards for achievement: students recognize mistakes, hear a wrong note, notice a missed entrance, and the student corrects them in order to achieve excellence in performance. Playing music teaches children to use a disciplined approach, establish sound standards, and strive for a high degree of excellence.

- **Setting Goals and Measuring Progress**

Studying music also teaches students to set goals and work towards them. Initially, the teacher measures both the goals and the progress towards them. But as children grow in independence and musicality, they learn to set their own goals and to determine for themselves how well they have achieved them. Each week they establish a goal for the following week, and each week they analyze their progress. When goals are not met, another approach may be called for, but the goal itself cannot be abandoned. Because music is mastered step-by-step, and because each step in the process is crucial, children can measure their progress and can experience a deep sense of achievement in mastering the elements of musicianship.

A father explains it this way:

> I think that playing music gives kids a chance to measure their success. There are standards. It's not subjective. Someone else is measuring your success and giving you regular feedback on how well you are meeting your goals. It's a one-on-one, individualized program for personalized goal setting.

There are all too few opportunities for this individualized, one-on-one mentoring today. The best person to give this kind of attention to children is a parent, but many parents have too little time to do this well. Teachers at school also do their best to provide this kind of attention, but usually they have too many students to be able to devote significant time or energy to any one student. Tutors or music teachers, however, are paid to give undivided attention to a single student, so they can attend to each child and each child's specific needs in this crucial way.

- **The Mathematics Connection**

A whole host of anecdotal evidence indicates that people who excel in music also excel in math. Think of Albert Einstein with his violin, Max Planck performing on the piano, or Richard Feynman with his bongo drums. So goes the old joke: "What do you have when you put four mathematicians in a room? A string quartet."

Until recently, it was impossible to show that music study was the cause of math ability (or math study the cause of music ability). But it did seem clear that these two disciplines appealed to the same kinds of minds.

Several recent studies imply a cause and effect relationship, suggesting that studying music actually improves children's skills in math. In one study, 237 second-grade children were divided into two groups. Both groups were given math instruction, but only one group received additional piano training. The group that had received piano training with their math instruction scored 27% higher on proportional math and fractions tests than children who used only the math software.[68]

More such studies are being performed today. A study by the United States Department of Education collected data on more than 25,000 secondary school students and found that students who were actively involved in instrumental music in middle school and high school showed "significantly higher levels of mathematic proficiency by grade 12." [69]

It is important to note that this correlation between music study and math performance applied regardless of the students' socio-economic level. In fact, one study looked at the most economically and socially disadvantaged students in eighth grade to see how their involvement in music and art might affect their overall achievement. The researchers found that the students involved in music out-performed their peers on standardized mathematics tests. In addition, it was found that the advantages enjoyed by the music students lasted and improved over time.[70]

- **Music Study and Spatial Reasoning**

Although people have talked for years about the connection between intelligence and music, it was only in 1993 that scientists at the University of California at Irvine attempted to document such a correlation. In what has come to be called "the Mozart effect," the researchers played Mozart's "Sonata for Two Pianos in D Major" (K448, to be exact) to undergraduate students. They found that students who heard 10 minutes of the Mozart sonata and then took an IQ test scored significantly higher (by nine points) on the test than they scored when they had listened to relaxation tapes or when they sat quietly and listened to nothing. Later, it was found that students listening to Mozart registered a short (15 minute) improvement in their spatial reasoning.[71]

Spatial reasoning is the ability to perceive the visual world accurately, to form mental images of objects, and recognize variations of those objects. This kind of reasoning, also called spatial-temporal reasoning, accounts for our ability to recognize, compare, and find relationships among patterns. People with good spatial-temporal aptitude can easily work mazes, draw geometric shapes, copy patterns of block designs, and fold paper into designated patterns. This ability is required for some kinds of mathematical problem-solving and scientific reasoning, and also for the game of chess.

Although these experimental results were not duplicated by other researchers at other institutions (and therefore lost some credibility), other experiments done on the Irvine campus have fared better. Researchers there tested preschoolers who had been given eight months of keyboard lessons and found that they showed a 46% boost in their spatial reasoning ability.[72] Other researchers found that preschoolers who received lessons on classroom instruments improved their spatial-temporal scores.[73] Three years later, another study compared children who were given piano lessons to children who received computer lessons, casual singing lessons, or no lessons at all. Again, researchers found that children who studied the piano demonstrated a significant and long-lasting gain in their spatial reasoning abilities, but the children who learned other skills showed no similar improvement.[74] These results were confirmed two years later in Wisconsin, when kindergarten children who were given music instruction scored 48% higher than those without music instruction on spatial-temporal skill tests.[75]

These scientific studies have begun to link music study and mathematical ability but, of course, much work remains to be done in order to explain how these connections function.

- **Other Connections Between Music and Academic Performance**

In addition to research showing that music improves a child's mathematical abilities, other studies around the world indicate that music also strengthens a child's verbal abilities. A recent Chinese study shows that school-age children who participated in music scored significantly higher on verbal memory tests than their classmates who had not.[76] Earlier studies done by the Chinese University of Hong Kong found that adults who had learned to play a musical instrument as children had a 16% better word memory than adults who had had no musical training.

According to a U.S. researcher, college music majors achieved higher reading scores than those in all other majors.[77] And a French researcher found that "comprehension of some aspects of language processing is improved by early musical training…children who had musical training…detected incongruities in language better than children who were not musically trained." [78] This phenomenon may be explained by the finding at Harvard University that special structures in the brain responsible for interpreting abstract ideas are also involved in music perception.

Other studies showed that, when compared to students who had not studied music, high school music students scored higher on the Scholastic Aptitude Test (the SAT), widely used by colleges in their admission process. One eight-year study showed that students who participated in All-State ensembles consistently scored more than 200 points higher on the SAT than non-music students.[79] Students in music performance scored 57 points higher on the verbal and 41 points higher on the math sections of the test. These results suggest that music study was even more beneficial for improved verbal performance than for math performance. [80]

Test results are one way of measuring academic success. Academic honors are another, more subjective indication of accomplishment. In this arena, too, music students excelled, receiving more academic honors and awards than non-music students. According to the National Center for Education Statistics, the percentage of music participants receiving A's and B's was significantly higher than the percentage of non-participants receiving those grades.[81]

Some studies suggest that music study can even help provide support for failing students and improve their schoolwork. In one controlled experiment in Providence, Rhode Island, 48 poorly-performing first-grade students in eight public schools were given a weekly, sequential music skills program. When they were tested later, it was found that the poorly performing students had caught up to the control group in reading and, even more remarkably, they had pulled ahead of the others in math. The authors of the study theorized that when students discover how pleasurable making music is, they become motivated to acquire musical skills. When students realize that they can learn challenging musical skills, their attitude towards learning other skills and school work improves. In addition, learning music skills forces mental "stretching" useful for intellectual imagination.[82]

Even when it comes to the academic performance of children with disabilities, music can help. Children with learning disabilities have shown growth through the use of music therapy. According to the *Music Educators Journal*, "Research supports connections between

Chapter Eleven: Academic And Intellectual Benefits Of Music Study

speech and singing, rhythm and motor behavior, memory for song and memory for academic material... to optimize the student's ability to learn and interact.[83]

It seems that, any way you measure it, students who study music have an academic edge over their non-musical peers.

- **Why Is This So?**

Educators know that fine-motor (or small muscle) skills and hand-eye coordination are vital to a young child's intellectual as well as physical development. Young children need to learn to make their fingers go where their eyes tell them to go. Psychologists and educators tell us that competence in these physical skills is a stepping stone to the later development of reading and writing fluency. Since playing a musical instrument calls for hours of exercising to develop manual dexterity and promote these fine-motor skills, children who practice their instruments develop better coordination. As a result, it is believed that they develop stronger reading and writing skills. It may be that early musical exercises train the brain for the mastery of reading and writing.

How do other researchers explain this connection between music and intellectual skills? Gordon L. Shaw, a pioneer in the field, believes that the experience of music enhances some natural brain pathways. He boldly claims, "Music improves the hardware in the brain for thinking." Based on brain imaging done at Harvard University's Medical School,[84] Dr. Shaw thinks that certain musical structures excite specialized brain circuits essential for decoding complex ideas. He says, "If you can do it when you learn music, it should carry over into other reasoning tasks."

- **"The Mozart Effect"**

Based on some impressive scientific studies, Don Campbell published, in 1997, a book called *The Mozart Effect,* which made stupendous claims for the positive effects of music, claiming that listening to Mozart could create geniuses. (The book also promised that listening to Mozart could cure a host of diseases.) Campbell's book spawned a whole industry that filled CD shelves with discs and tapes of Mozart's music dedicated to making babies smarter and enhancing genius and health. Campbell (who trademarked the term "Mozart effect") has himself released several series of CD's and claims that they can boost creativity, imagination, intelligence, and healing.

Campbell's book started the make-your-baby-smart-with-music movement complete with music appreciation classes for infants. Varying in their approach and their quality, such classes are now being offered by music schools, community arts programs, and college music departments, as well as by independent teachers. It has become commonplace for young mothers to bring their year-old toddlers to introductory music classes. This emphasis on exposing babies to classical music has also been encouraged by politicians like those in Florida who lobbied to require state-funded preschools to play Mozart sonatas every day, and by a former governor of Georgia, who had tapes of Mozart's music issued to all new mothers.

Many detractors, claiming that Campbell exaggerated the benefits of the original research, call him a musical P.T. Barnum. Even before Campbell's popularization of the idea, there were many anecdotal stories about how music made people smarter, and a lot of it was just silly. What is new and undeniably compelling today is a wealth of solid empirical evidence showing that infants are born with neural mechanisms devoted exclusively to music[85] and that studying music enhances brain development and function. This new evidence is based on well-performed, tightly controlled scientific behavioral studies combined with cutting-edge neurological brain research. Because of the results of this ground-breaking research, there is now good reason to claim that music not only improves academic performance, but can also actively contribute to brain development, thereby boosting intelligence.

- **Neurological Studies**

Based on brain-imaging studies, scientists today agree that music training "grows" the brain in response to music the way a muscle grows in response to exercise. According to David Epstein, a conductor and composer at MIT, the experience of rhythm actually has a biological basis, and our understanding of music is grounded in the brain's experience of the body's natural rhythms.[86]

A California neurologist has another explanation. He argues that people who use their hands with great precision (and musicians certainly qualify) are privy to a way of knowing about the world that is inaccessible to those not schooled in manual arts. The hand's knowledge actually teaches the brain new tricks and can rewire the brain's neural circuitry.[87]

In Belgium, researchers have performed brain scans showing that one region in musicians' brains is larger than that of non-musicians. Musicians' brains also have a thicker bundle of nerve fibers connecting the two halves of the brain than do non-musicians, and that bundle of nerves in the brains of musicians is up to 15% larger. Expert musicians have a cerebellum (the part of the brain containing 70% of the brain's neurons) that is 5 % larger than that of non-musicians, and it is even larger in those musicians who began their training before the age of seven. These researchers also found, less surprisingly, that in musicians, the part of the brain associated with hearing contains 130% more gray matter than that of non-musicians.[88]

Even without these brain-scan studies, it seems obvious that studying music teaches children to develop the ability to understand and use symbols in new contexts, and these are skills crucial to mathematics and to abstract thinking. According to one expert, the very best engineers and technical designers in the Silicon Valley industry are, nearly without exception, practicing musicians.[89] Though this is another example of anecdotal evidence, it is compelling.

Tests of other intellectual functions found that the brains of musicians are in some ways more efficient than those of non-musicians. While pianists and non-musicians were asked to perform complex sequences of finger movements, their brains were scanned to determine the activity levels of brains cells. The researchers found that the musicians required less brain activity, or effort, to perform the same movements. Evidently the brains of pianists had become more efficient at making skilled finger movements as their brain functioning had been enhanced.[90]

In his book *A User's Guide to the Brain*, Dr. John Ratey explains what he believes is a key factor in the musician's intellectual abilities: musicians must do many things simultaneously. He writes, "The musician is constantly adjusting decisions on tempo, tone, style, rhythm, phrasing, and feeling—training the brain to become incredibly good at organizing and conducting numerous activities at once. Dedicated practice of this orchestration can have a great payoff for lifelong attentional skills, intelligence, and an ability for self-knowledge and expression." [91]

Added to this extensive list of the intellectual advantages of participating in music, considerable evidence indicates that participating in music is correlated with long-term career success. In fact, most Nobel Prize winners and members of the National Academy of Sciences enjoy music or art-related hobbies. According to researchers, the best way to predict success in *any* field is not high intelligence, test scores, or high-school grades, but rather participation as an adolescent in "challenging leisure-time activities," especially music performance and composition! Perhaps this is because performing music requires energy, self-motivation, and task commitment, all attributes that spur career and life success.[92] Reflecting on his own personal experience, the president of the ETS (the Educational Testing Service of SAT fame) said,

> The things I learned from my experience in music...are discipline, perseverance, dependability, composure, courage, and pride in results...not a bad preparation for the workforce![93]

Scientists are just now exploring the secrets of our wonderfully engineered brains, but it seems clear that musical training improves them and increases our intellectual capacity. Based on new research, it looks like the old stories about the connection between intelligence and musical training contained more than a grain of truth.

CHAPTER TWELVE

THE SOCIAL AND PERSONAL BENEFITS OF STUDYING MUSIC

The enormous benefits of music study for children of all races and ethnicities are becoming better known as studies around the world demonstrate scientifically what has long been said anecdotally: playing an instrument is good for you. In the last chapter we examined the correlation between music study and intelligence. In this chapter we will look at the surprising and sometimes dramatic connections that have been found between studying music and a child's social life, character, and emotional well-being.

Social Life

1) Belonging to a Group

Belonging to an orchestra can provide teenagers with a group of regular friends. Several parents admitted starting their children in music simply because they wanted to enlarge their children's social circle. One mother shared her thinking:

> Kelly is a very quiet kid and I wanted to get her a quiet activity at school to keep her involved. I had been in choir when I was in high school and I liked it, so that's how I started thinking about music for her. It worked. In her orchestra she found a good group of friends.

Everybody needs to have a place in society, to fit in somehow. If you play an instrument in a group, you belong. Teen-agers seeking their identity need to feel that they fill an important slot somewhere. Those who play an instrument, especially an instrument like the bass, bassoon or French horn, are vitally important to the orchestra they play in. Because the orchestra needs them, they "matter," and feeling that you matter is significant for a child's healthy psychological and emotional development. When everything works well in a chamber group or in an orchestra, participants feel tremendous joy. The act of belonging to a group, contributing something unique, and feeling that the group is greater than the sum of its parts, gives young people a sense of self-esteem and an awareness that they are part of something grand. This is heady stuff.

Within the family, playing a unique instrument gives each child something that no one else in the family can do well, distinguishing them from their siblings and creating an exclusive identity. Especially when a younger child is struggling with a persistently successful older sibling, playing an instrument can give the younger child a sense of personal accomplishment and help him or her carve out a unique identity.

2) A "Good Crowd"

The kind of group to which children belong is vitally important—to children and to parents. To a lot of parents, it is the "goodness" of the group that matters. Parents want their child to belong to "a good crowd."

A Chicago mother explains:

> Now my kid has friends that I am happy to have him hang around with. These musical friends have been different—they're more serious about school. Most of the kids in the band are in the top 10% of the school academically. Maybe their seriousness about music rolled over onto other things.

A parent in upstate New York said she didn't have to worry about her son because of his music:

> He had friends who had gotten into trouble, but he told me, "Mom, you don't have to worry—I don't do those things." Because he knows he can't afford to mess around with the kind of practice time he has to put in. He's developed high standards that help keep him on the straight and narrow.

3) Music as a Civilizing Force

This mother's feelings are well supported by research studies showing that secondary students who participated in band or orchestra were the least likely to use alcohol, tobacco, or illicit drugs.[94] Other research found that high school music students were less likely to skip classes, get suspended, drop out of school, or get arrested.[95]

The idea that studying music civilizes the young is not new. Benny Goodman's father, in the 1920's, decided to teach his sons to play an instrument because it was thought that music tamed the wildness out of boys who might turn to crime, that "boys who were practicing trumpets and drums were not out shoplifting."[96] This is one reason boys' bands were so popular in New York in the 1920's.

Criminal records today show that the more a person is involved in music, the lower his arrest record.[97] Much, however, depends on the *kind* of music that kids play. Rap and hip-hop artists have been associated too often with anti-social behavior. It seems, however, that when classical music is played, the criminal element runs for cover! This sounds wacky, but it is true. The city of Vallejo, California, suffered from a tough reputation until the police started using loudspeakers to broadcast operatic arias and classical music into a "seedy" part of downtown.[98] This music helped revitalize the downtown area, chasing away drug dealers and prostitutes who fled the sounds of Bach and Beethoven. Police in other cities claim classical music discourages the young from loitering and, if the young aren't hanging out on a particular corner, neither will the hookers and drug dealers. If classical music can protect an area of town by effectively clearing out a drug den, can it work to provide protection for our children? It sure sounds goofy, but now we have evidence that classical music can ward off "bad" influences.

4) Learning Teamwork

Young musicians, like soccer players or thespians, develop team-building skills, learning to work in harmony with others towards a common goal. Participating in an orchestra requires a player to demonstrate perfectly timed coordination. Chamber music requires precise cooperation and exquisite sensitivity to other people. A group cannot play music well without a high level of joint effort and team work. As a result, making music teaches young people how to interact well with others.

5) Learning about the World

Another advantage of youth orchestras is that they expand the horizons of teenagers, introducing them to young people of different ethnicities and cultures. Because youth orchestras often travel to perform, youngsters get to travel to countries they might never have visited on their own. Kids from Nebraska get to go to New York, kids from New York get to go to Australia, and kids from Chicago get to go to Ireland. Seeing Tokyo with its wildly appreciative teen-age audiences throwing them flowers is something high-school orchestra students will never forget. As one mother said, "Eric's French horn wound up taking him to Lithuania with his orchestra. I mean, it's incredible where that horn has taken him."

Not only in school, but also later in life, music can serve as a way to meet people with similar interests. Seeking others with whom to play in chamber groups, adult musicians have a ready avenue for socializing with new people. One amateur cellist reported that when she travels abroad, she connects with local people through the music world and enjoys experiencing a new culture through her classical music connections.

"Music has a great power for bringing people together," said Ted Turner of the Turner Broadcasting System. Putting it in a humanitarian and political context, he added, "With so many forces in this world acting to drive wedges between people, it's important to preserve these things that help us experience our common humanity." [99]

Character-Building Benefits

Character-building is a dated educational concept. Today's students are more likely to be taught "values clarification," a process of working through their own feelings to discover what they personally believe to be right and wrong. But solid values do help form a healthy, productive person and are crucial for making decisions. While clarifying personal beliefs is important, so are a number of skills once considered part of character education. There is no need to sacrifice character for values—a whole person needs both. Music study promotes several of the skills fundamental to building character: how to be engaged and take action, make decisions and solve problems, construct a work ethic, tolerate delayed gratification, manage personal time, and discipline oneself. All parents want their children to have these skills.

1)   Active Engagement

Playing an instrument offers a child a dynamic, kinetic activity as opposed to passive pastimes like watching television. It involves "doing" rather than "watching others do." One's thoughts must be smoothly transformed into action; one's physical movements must be precisely calibrated in order to produce the correct tone and timing. Music-makers are actively engaged, using both mind and body. Musicians cannot be couch potatoes.

2)   Decision Making and Problem Solving

Studying music requires making many decisions continuously and simultaneously. What fingering to use? How hard to press? How long to practice? When to try a new technique? How to achieve a desired effect? Asking these questions, devising answers, trying them out, and then reworking the answers, are all exercises in making decisions and solving problems. According to the Center for Timing, Coordination, and Motor Skills, children who understand complex rhythms make faster and better decisions, both physically and academically.[100] The skills acquired in musical decision-making are then easily transferred to the larger world where many other kinds of decisions must be made.

Solutions to musical problems demand higher-order thinking skills: analyzing, creating a product, focusing on a result, improvising, and assessing outcomes. Spending hours making musical decisions and solving musical problems develops important problem-solving skills which can be successfully applied to many other endeavors.

3)   Work Ethic

Pursuing music teaches a healthy work ethic. With poorly developed work habits, many children—at all socioeconomic levels—fail in school and on the job. That work matters was obvious to previous generations of American children who helped out on their parents' farms, but it is a lesson harder to come by in today's world. Today's children may understand the connection between basketball practice

Chapter Twelve: The Social And Personal Benefits Of Studying Music

and athletic success, but, as school teachers can attest, children do not automatically understand that there is a connection between studying and getting good grades.

However, in music as in sports, success is clearly defined. Playing an instrument cannot be mastered without work, and working on music gives clear results. Children can see the ball go into the basket. They can hear the right note played. They receive immediate and unequivocal confirmation of their efforts through their senses. This teaches children the important lesson that work does indeed pay off. It encourages students to stick with a task through boredom and technical difficulties until they master the material, achieve success, and develop a robust work ethic.

Learning "stick-to-it-iveness" from music, children can then apply it to their efforts in other areas and so develop commitment to their undertakings. They often become better athletes and students because they have learned to persevere. Once they achieve success—and they will—they can be justifiably proud of themselves for what they have accomplished through hard work. This leads to internalized self-esteem, a trait much prized today.

4)   Delaying Gratification

Learning to tolerate delayed gratification is an especially important lesson in today's super-fast world of immediate information retrieval, instant oatmeal, and split-second video games. Children who learn to persevere and not give up when the going gets tough develop a tolerance for delayed gratification. They have experienced frustration and overcome it. They can forego immediate rewards and wait for the bigger pay off. This quality used to be called "patience," and it was considered a virtue for centuries. Although it has lost some of its luster as a virtue, patience has enormous importance in building character.

Even with microwave ovens and broad-band communication, some things still take time. Children who learn to play a musical instrument know how to wait and work toward success, one small step at a time. They have enormous advantages over those who have never learned this vital lesson.

5) Time Management

Making music requires putting in hours of practice. As a result, all teen-age musicians, of necessity, learn the art of time management. Music students become better able to plan, sequence, and coordinate their daily activities.[101] Studying music helps students develop skills for organizing time and using it well. They must decide what is and what is not important, and they must understand their bodily needs to determine under what conditions they do their best work. I remember the day my son discovered that he needed to start the day with a particularly unpleasant flute exercise. If he neglected to do the exercise early in the morning, he couldn't get his body to do it later in the day. Every morning after that, the high, piercing long tone of Jonathan's flute would be my shrill 6:00 AM alarm.

6) Self-Discipline

Music teaches simple self-discipline. It is not easy to practice scales when more attractive activities beckon. Many parents told me that their children had learned self-control through the study of music. They said that music had taught their children to focus, to surmount problems, and to cope creatively with difficult social and academic issues. The self-discipline they learned in music made it possible for them to accomplish in other areas as well. The National Commission on Music Education recognizes this in their statement:

> As a child begins to understand the connection between hours of practice and the quality of a performance, self-discipline becomes self-reinforcing. It is only a short jump from that realization to making the connection between self-discipline and performance in life.[102]

7) Risk Taking

Advancing in the field of music requires performers to address their fears—especially the fear of failure. Dealing with fear is important for success in any field. All of us experience "performance anxiety" during our careers and in our daily lives, and a little anxiety can be a good thing if we have learned how to make it work in our favor. Dealing with anxiety early and frequently enough to de-fang its sting empowers us later in life. According to researchers, children who perform music learn to overcome shyness and performance fear. They learn to deal with their anxiety and to be less fearful of failure.

Music students learn to take risks. Performers take risks every time they pick up their instruments. If they make a mistake, people will hear it and in rehearsal they will be publicly corrected. They know that mistakes will occur and that recognizing errors and thrashing them out is an essential part of the music-making process. Being able to take correction without feeling humiliated requires the kind of maturity that not every adult can display. But instrumentalists learn to do this gracefully if they are to survive. It is a crucial lesson for success in any field, and music performance teaches this life-enhancing skill.

8) Dealing with Disappointments

Young musicians also learn to accept defeats and to take them in stride. When a student orchestra forms, the players are arranged in order of performance excellence: first chair goes to the best player, second chair goes to the next best, and so on. Therefore, to sit in an orchestra requires being judged and accepting one's assigned seating placement. In addition to auditioning for their orchestras (and re-auditioning each year for their placement within the orchestra), students compete for scholarships and orchestral honors such as solo concerto performances. Many more performers audition than will win parts. The odds can be as high as 30 to 1, making music far more competitive than athletics. Most musicians who audition, even those who are excellent, will win nothing.

The father of a clarinetist thinks that the experience of competing has been valuable and highly educational for his son. He says,

> Auditioning and competing with others is a good way for kids to grow in self-confidence. Traveling to auditions and competitions and performances, even when they don't win, even when they don't do well, even when they feel bad about it... It's a good way for them to learn. Kids learn to steel their nerves, to take chances, to accept losses. It builds character and they come out stronger for it.

Other parents echo this father's belief in the positive value of these challenging experiences. The mother of an accomplished cellist said,

> The first year Dena didn't make Governor's School she was very disappointed. But then she *did* make it the next year. That's perseverance. I learned this quality from my daughter! She says every audition makes you that much better. You are that much stronger. To get up in front of someone who is looking at you with a critical eye, who is testing you, lets you know how much the music is your own and how much you are your own person.

Perseverance is hard to teach. A mother from North Carolina lost heart when she heard her son say, "Maybe I should give up. I played my heart out and still didn't make it, so maybe I should quit. Maybe I'm not good enough." But he didn't quit. He kept at it through his disappointment until he *did* make it. His mother is most proud of how he learned to persevere.

9) Dealing with Loss

All musicians will sometimes (and usually often) experience the disappointment of "losing." How to lose gracefully is an important life skill and it is one that we will all need many times in our lives. However, in schools today, especially elementary schools, "competition" is a dirty word and is discouraged. Instead, schools urge cooperation. It is believed that all children are "winners" and should therefore win, or at least, not lose. It is thought that winning builds self-esteem. While the motivation for this attitude is understandable, the effect it has on children is to deprive them of experiences that teach them to lose well and not lose heart. Musicians have ample opportunity to learn that losing is not a permanent condition, and that after loss will come many other chances for success.

The mother of a violinist recounts what her son learned from his auditioning:

> Kids learn that they can have good days and they can have bad days, just like athletes or any other performers. When my son auditioned for his local orchestra, he won the first chair and his friend, a nice young lady, was second chair. When the two friends auditioned for another orchestra at the Illinois Music Educators Association performance, he got second chair and that young lady played first. When I asked him what happened, he shrugged and said, "Who knows? But it's OK. She's pretty good."

Through this process, children learn that there will always be another opportunity. They learn that life is not always fair. In other words, they learn to lose gracefully.

The most important lesson children learn is that they may not succeed as they had hoped to or expected to, and it may hurt, but they will live. And they will live with a slightly thicker skin and a much greater depth of understanding. This is called maturity.

Personal and Emotional Benefits

1) Poise

Standing in front of others to speak or perform may be cause for panic in otherwise unflappable professionals. Many careers and even hobbies require some ability to stand up, face an audience, and say what must be said. Even hosting a formal party may require some kind of public speaking. The organization "Toastmasters," for example, was formed to help adults get over "stage fright."

Performing music can help develop poise. Learning as a child to address an audience, to perform with minimal anxiety, and to cope in difficult situations is another gift of the study of music.

2) Self Expression

Music is an avenue for self-expression, allowing children to express themselves and to share their feelings with others. It can allow children to give voice to that dark part of themselves that they suppress in day-to-day life. This mother of a Florida violist said,

> My son is usually very mild mannered. But there's something that I don't understand going on in him when he picks up the viola. It's like his alter ego. There's this other part of him that is very strong and aggressive and only comes out when he plays.

The mother of a clarinetist agrees:

> There is literally a change that comes over Will when he begins to play. He becomes a different person. You can see in his face that he is completely absorbed and is living inside of his music. He moves differently, he blocks everything else out—he doesn't see that there are other people out there. He loses himself and I see his soul coming through. It's not just an intellectual exercise because there isn't any intellectualization. It's just him and his soul.

A California mother claims that her children can better express themselves because of their musical training. She says,

> My kids think differently than my husband and I do. They see life in a different way. They write well and express themselves well because of how they learned to express themselves through music. You know how they say music is a language? Well, it's a language that lets things get said that can't be said in regular words.

3)   Healing and Emotional Outlet

As a minimum, playing music is simply a very nice hobby. It's a pleasant way to spend time, a way to entertain oneself. Unlike team sports, which most people give up after college, music is a hobby that can be practiced well into old age, providing a lifetime of pleasurable activity and seeing a person through good times and bad.

Music can be relaxing. General Norman Schwarzkopf said,

> During the Gulf War, the few opportunities I had for relaxation, I always listened to music, and it brought to me great peace of mind...I have shared my love of music with people throughout the world...and all of this started with the music I was taught in a third-grade elementary class in Princeton, New Jersey.[103]

This quality is perhaps responsible for the increasingly frequent reports from the medical world demonstrating that "music has a healing effect on patients"[104] and that people who participate in the arts live longer.[104] Researchers have found that giving the elderly music lessons makes them healthier.

Certainly, we know that playing music provides an emotional outlet. Films and literature offer abundant portraits of people soulfully assuaging their *angst* at the piano or the violin. Playing music certainly provides a healthier release than alcohol, drugs, or promiscuous sex.

The mother of a Utah violinist mused,

> Kass is emotionally stronger because of her music. If she is struggling at basketball practice, she comes home and plays violin for an hour and emerges a different person. She often uses her violin to cope with stress and sadness. When her grandmother was very sick, she would go to her room, close the door, and play for hours.

4) Self-Respect

Making music develops pride, self-respect, and self-esteem, qualities highly valued by educators and psychologists since they promote intellectual and emotional growth as well as character development. Although we hear a great deal about how important it is for children to develop self-esteem, we don't hear much about how to actually help them do it. It is mistakenly thought that children acquire self-esteem by receiving abundant praise and support from their parents and teachers. There is, however, no scientific evidence that we develop self-esteem from being told how good we are. In and of itself, positive feedback does little, since children who receive unwarranted praise can easily dismiss it. However, receiving praise after accomplishing something difficult like performing a Mozart sonata generates genuine pride, deep self-respect, and true self-esteem.

People acquire self-esteem from doing something that not every Tom, Dick, and Harriet can do. Achieving and demonstrating competence in music, receiving both pleasure and praise, can result in solid and healthy self-appreciation. Indeed, researchers in New York City found that students who participated in arts programs showed significantly increased self-esteem (and thinking skills).[106]

Parents can't do scientific studies on their children, of course, but they do see the same effect. One mother said,

> Being a teenager is tough. Teen-agers are on an emotional roller coaster ride. But music has built Olivia's confidence, especially since she receives praise from people outside of her family. When strangers compliment her, it means more than when I tell her how good she is. Applause matters and appreciation fans her self-esteem.

Another mother offers this highly subjective example:

> If you've sat in on an orchestra rehearsal or in the house listening to your kids practice and then attend the performance and you see that big smile on their faces at the end of the concert, you know how good music makes these kids feel about themselves!

5)   Feelings of Validation

There is another, largely overlooked, explanation for how music study enhances a child's self-esteem. It has to do with parental effort and investment.

Parents who provide their children with a quality musical education make tangible efforts and significant sacrifices in time and money. Children witnessing these sacrifices realize their parents must care deeply about them. They feel acknowledged and "validated" by their parents' investment in them. This kind of parental support goes deeper than the formulaic "I love you" uttered mechanically at the end of telephone calls. Based not simply on words, but also on real deeds, such demonstrations of parental support truly enhance a child's self esteem. "If my parents are willing to do so much for me, I must be worthy of it," they think.

6)   Self-Awareness, Self-Reflection, and Simple Attention

Music also teaches self-awareness and self-reflection. A New York mother said,

> Music is a kind of metaphor for my daughter's life. If she stays calm when she plays the violin, she stays calm in her life. Playing gives her the opportunity to learn about herself and what she is capable of. It helps her to be a better person because she knows how to sit and think about what she's doing.

These parents' personal feelings about how music affected their children's emotional lives were given scientific validity by researchers who studied how to meet the needs of disadvantaged children. The researchers found "significant increases in overall self-concept of at-risk children participating in an arts program that included music." [107]

One simple reason for this is that performing music is a healthy way to get some good old-fashioned attention. Every child (and adult for that matter) needs a certain amount of attention from others.

Performing, being the "center of attention," standing in the limelight (sometimes on stage), having others look at you and listen to your music, and being appreciated for your performance— all of these experiences are extremely gratifying. Disadvantaged and at-risk children are particularly in need of getting this kind of attention for their behavior.

7) Pure Pleasure

The above is already a pretty impressive list of benefits that music bestows on its practitioners. Of all the benefits of music, however, the most important one is this: music simply gives pleasure. Enormous pleasure. Music gives self-gratifying pleasure to the performer while giving delight to others. What a marvelous and fortuitous combination of joys!

A clarinetist's mother put it this way:

> How can you not be thrilled for your kid when you see that Christmas-morning excitement on his face as he walks in to practice with his youth symphony? He still has that look when they give him a new piece of music! Way too many people you encounter today, they wish their entire life away. My kid is only 13, and he already has work that he loves.

A father who spent his entire corporate severance package on a violin for his daughter explained why he was willing to do it:

> It was just the joy that I saw on her face when she was making music. I don't know how to describe it, other than…there was rapture. You could see it when she played. Pride, a sense of accomplishment, beauty… I don't know, just joy, pure and simple.

Music does that for all of us—different kinds of music for different people in different places at different times—but music gives people pleasure. All human beings respond to music with strong emotion and palpable joy.

Chapter Twelve: The Social And Personal Benefits Of Studying Music

Plato, who theorized extensively about music, wrote, "Music is a more potent instrument than any other for education, because rhythm and harmony find their way into the inward places of the soul." Music lifts the soul and elevates us. It can be an intense emotional and spiritual experience. Many parents feel that music connects their children with the spiritual realm. There can be a kind of religious quality to the performance of music.

Some parents say that this spiritual sense derives from the tradition inherent in music performance. There is a repertoire and there are things to know and these things are being passed down— the mantle is being passed on—from older generations to younger ones. The young are being prepared to take over their role and to assume their place for the future. They see themselves as a link in the great chain of music making. This gives a formal, celebratory, religious quality to the whole endeavor of music. Music elevates us and distinguishes human beings from other creatures.

The United States Secretary of Education, Richard W. Riley, reflecting on the manifest benefits of music, wrote, "Casals says that music fills him with the wonder of life and the 'incredible marvel' of being a human. Ives says it expands his mind and challenges him to be a true individual. Bernstein says it is enriching and ennobling...Studying music and the arts elevates children's education, expands students' horizons, and teaches them to appreciate the wonder of life." [108]

Others go further. They say simply, "Music gives life meaning."

APPENDIX

OVERVIEW OF THE ORCHESTRA

How many musicians are required to create an orchestra? Between 15 and 120, depending on the specific requirements of the music. It can be quite a large group! Whereas a Mozart symphony can be played with as few as 15 musicians, a Mahler symphony may call for as many as 120. For the most part, the instruments that contemporary performers play today have pretty much remained the same since the 1830's, when the modern orchestra took shape.

Orchestral instruments can be divided into four groups or "sections": strings, woodwinds, brass, and percussion. Every family of instruments shares structural features, but each instrument in the orchestra has its own distinctive sound. The words used to describe music borrow from the language of the visual arts. Thus we speak of a middle C note played by different instruments as having a different quality or "color." Composers use these colors to "paint" their compositions in a process known as "orchestration." Certain composers, for example Ravel, are known for their genius at orchestration, for using just the right instrument or combination of instruments for each effect they wish to create.

THE STRING SECTION

The string family of instruments is by far the largest group in the orchestra. It consists of the violins, violas, cellos (also called "celli"— the Italian plural), and basses, all of which have four strings and share the same basic shape and design. The looser, thicker, and longer the string—the lower the note. The strings that these instruments are named for are called "catgut" but they were originally made, not from cats, but from the intestines of sheep or goats. Today, almost all strings are made of metal. Strings vibrate when they are plucked by a player's fingers or stroked by a bow made from hundreds of strands of hair from horses' tails. This produces sound. The biology of string construction may seem unappetizing, but the combination of animal gut and horse hair has produced some of the world's most exquisite music.

All string players, even if they are left handed, use the fingers of their left hand to depress the string in order to change its length, and therefore the pitch, of the note. They use their right hand to draw the bow across the string and make it sing. When the bow is drawn across a string that is not depressed at all (the string is "open"), the string is at its greatest length and so produces the lowest possible note. As the player's fingers shorten the string, the notes produced become higher and higher.

Before they play, string players rub the hair of the bow with a sticky substance called "rosin" or "resin"(made of fir tree sap) which roughens the hair, giving the bow a better "grip" on the strings.

- **VIOLIN**

In an orchestra, there are two sections of violins, the "firsts" and the "seconds." Each section has a "principal player," (often called simply the "principal") who leads his or her section. The principal of the first violin section is also the "concertmaster" who serves as the ensemble leader and represents the entire orchestra. Following a performance, the conductor shakes the hand of the concertmaster in symbolic recognition of the work of the entire orchestra.

The violin section is the largest one in the orchestra. The smallest member of the string family, the violin is made of more than 50 pieces of wood glued together in a highly technical process. The violin has four strings; G is the lowest string, followed by D, A and E. The violin bow, a very important part of the instrument, is flexible

Appendix: Overview of the Orchestra

and has a slight curve. An extremely expressive instrument, the violin can produce sounds that are delicate as well as fierce. Of all orchestral instruments, the violin most closely resembles the human voice and emotions.

- **VIOLA**

The viola is slightly larger than the violin in all dimensions and produces a lower, richer, more sonorous sound. Its strings are slightly thicker than violin strings and are tuned from C to G to D to A. Its bow, though a bit heavier and sturdier, is very similar to that of the violin. With its somewhat mournful sound, the viola is used almost exclusively in classical music.

- **CELLO**

The cello's proper name is the "violoncello." It is so much larger than the viola that it cannot be held under a player's chin like its violin and viola cousins, but must be placed with one end on the floor, so that cellists hold the instrument between their knees to play it. The cello is held in place on the floor by a pin, a steel spike extending to the floor from the bottom of the cello. The instrument's sound is one octave deeper than the viola. The cello has a very wide range, and its strings are tuned from C to G, D, and A like the strings of the viola. Some people (primarily cellists) insist that it is the cello with its rich, mellow tone, rather than the violin that most closely resembles the human voice.

- **BASS**

The bass, also called the "double bass," "contra bass," or "string bass," is the largest member of the string family and has the deepest and most resonant sound. It is called "double," not because there are two of them or because it is twice as large as another instrument, but because the bass instrument was often assigned to play the same notes as the cellos, but an octave lower, thereby "doubling" the note. (The term "double" now refers to the octave below. Other instruments—the double bassoon, for example—were similarly named, and for the same reason.) The string bass, despite its large size, is a delicate instrument. The bass is tuned in fourths and has E, A, D, and G strings. Bass players usually stand or perch themselves on a high stool in order to play their instrument.

THE WOODWIND SECTION

Woodwind instruments are called "wood" winds because they were originally made of wood and they are played with "wind," which the players create by blowing. Today these instruments are made not only of wood, but also of fine metals, plastic, horn and ivory. The woodwinds make more uniquely distinctive sounds than any other family of instruments.

All of the woodwinds are shaped into long, narrow pipes studded with rows of holes. These instruments have levers that are depressed in order to open and close the holes in the piping. The levers and keys are necessary because, to create the requisite sounds, these holes in the pipes must be placed in positions that would be awkward for fingers to reach. One end of the lever is convenient for the finger and the other end covers the hole. The more holes that are covered, the longer the active section of pipe becomes, and the longer the pipe, the lower the note sounds.

When the woodwind players blow into their pipes, the air inside the instrument vibrates, and this vibrating air makes the sounds we hear. The woodwinds consist of four basic instruments: flute, oboe, clarinet, and bassoon, which are usually grouped together in the middle of the orchestra. Each has its unique sound or "color."

The woodwind family shares several physical characteristics. These instruments (with the exception of the flute) use one or two "reeds," which are made up of thin slices of bamboo or "cane" (a tall grass grown in southern Europe). The clarinet has one reed attached to its mouthpiece and so is dubbed a "single reed" instrument. When the clarinetist blows into the instrument, the reed vibrates to create sound. The oboe has two thin reeds in its mouthpiece, making it a "double reed" instrument. (Actually, a double reed is one reed, but it

Appendix: Overview of the Orchestra

is bent over, sliced in two, and tied around a hollow tube.) The player blows between these two reeds, making them vibrate. A cousin of the oboe is the English horn which is larger than the oboe and lower in pitch. (This is a peculiarly named instrument, since the English horn is not a horn nor is it English.) Like the oboe, the bassoon and the English horn are double reed instruments.

- **FLUTE (AND PICCOLO)**

The flute was originally made of wood but today it is usually made of silver, although some modern flutes are made of gold or platinum. Unlike the other woodwinds, which are played in the upright position, the flute is played horizontally and is sometimes called the "transverse" flute for this reason. The flute is also distinct from other woodwinds in how its sound is produced. Whereas the other woodwind players make sound by blowing into their instruments, the flutist blows across the instrument—actually across an open hole—and so produces a sound in the same way that a whistle is produced by blowing across the mouth of an open beer bottle. The flute has a large, three-octave range. It has a pure, heavenly tone and is sometimes visualized as a thin silver ribbon of sound.

The piccolo, essentially a baby flute, (it is half the size of a flute) plays the highest and the shrillest notes in the orchestra. Its sound is one octave higher than the flute. The piccolo and the flute have such similar fingering that the piccolo is easily mastered by flute players, giving them two instruments to play in an orchestra. A flutist who plays both instruments is said to "double" on the piccolo. In professional orchestras, players who "double" are often paid double for their efforts.

- **OBOE (AND ENGLISH HORN)**

The word "oboe" comes from the French word "hautbois" or "loud wind instrument." The oboe has a strong and nasal quality, which makes it stand out from all other orchestral instruments. Because of this quality, and because the oboe had the most stable pitch in the orchestra historically, the oboe is the instrument to which the entire

211

orchestra tunes. The oboe's "A" sounds at exactly 440 vibrations per second.

The oboist holds the instrument in front of the body with the player's arms in a natural position and uses the fingers to open and close the holes along the length of the instrument. Within the orchestra, this unique instrument is very much in demand. (The oboe is not frequently used outside of symphony orchestras, so it is much less in demand for performing other kinds of music.) Since learning to master the oboe is time-consuming and difficult, good oboists are relatively rare. In the professional world, an outstanding oboist is handsomely rewarded in both prestige and salary.

Related to the oboe is the English horn, which is a kind of contralto oboe with a thick reed. The English horn is tuned to a perfect fifth in pitch below the oboe, but is played and fingered like the oboe so an accomplished oboist can easily play it.

- **CLARINET**

The clarinetist holds the instrument, like the oboist does, in front of the body. The standard orchestral clarinet is called the B-flat clarinet, although the A clarinet is also used in orchestral works. (There used to be a third kind, a C clarinet, which is no longer used.) The various clarinets look quite similar, but the A clarinet is longer and its sound is a half-step lower in pitch than the B-flat clarinet. The B-flat clarinet sounds a B-flat when C is fingered; the A clarinet sounds an A when the C is fingered. The reason for having clarinets in different pitches is that, when a piece contains numerous accidentals (sharps or flats), the player can simply switch to an instrument that is keyed differently, eliminating the need to deal with the complexity of the accidentals.

Rounding out the clarinet family are a) the bass clarinet which is larger, is pitched an octave lower than the standard instrument and is quite expensive to purchase; b) the E-flat clarinet which is smaller than the others, sounds in a very high register, and is played in both orchestral and band music; and c) the alto clarinet. All of these

Appendix: Overview of the Orchestra

instruments, however, have the same fingering, so the clarinet player is comfortable with and proficient on all of them.

The clarinet has great expressiveness and dynamic range. Clarinet notes sound different according to their range: the low notes of the clarinet sound silky and rich, the middle notes are smooth and slippery, and the upper notes can be piercing. The clarinet has a great deal of flexibility, and is heard outside of the symphony orchestra in a wide range of music styles from jazz to klezmer.

- **BASSOON (AND DOUBLE BASSOON)**

The bassoon is a versatile instrument in its range and in its repertoire. The lowest and longest of the woodwinds, the bassoon has to be folded over to reduce its length to four feet. This makes it more manageable for the player, who holds it diagonally. The bassoon has a very wide range of sound— four octaves. It sounds rich and dark in its low tones, and plaintive in its higher range. The double bassoon, sometimes called a "contrabassoon," is even larger and heavier, twice the length of the standard bassoon. It is played one octave lower than the standard bassoon and reaches the lowest notes of the entire orchestra. The bassoon, which has a deeply serious sound, can also be a fast-moving and agile instrument. These two conflicting characteristics can make the bassoon sound humorous.

When people speak of the woodwinds, however, they usually mean the four basic instruments, the clarinet, oboe, bassoon and flute. The more specialized members of the woodwind family—the English horn, double bassoon, and the piccolo—are played only when a specific piece of orchestral music calls for them.

THE BRASS SECTION

The brass section, at least, is well named, since these instruments are indeed made of brass (an alloy of copper and zinc) or other metals plated with copper or silver and usually polished to a high-gloss. The brass section consists primarily of the trumpet, French horn, trombone, and tuba. All the brass instruments are essentially long tubes, bent and twisted into shapes that make them easier to handle. Brass instruments, like woodwinds, use wind (the players' breath) to make air vibrate. Instead of relying on reeds like the woodwinds do, brass players use their own lips to create the vibrations. Their term for vibrating the lips is "buzzing."

Whereas woodwind instruments use levers that open and close holes to produce higher or lower notes, brass instruments accomplish this through the use of valves or slides. The valves on the trumpet, French horn, and the tuba open up extra lengths of tubing for avenues of sound. The length of the tube opened determines how low a note is sounded. Brass players also use specific lip positions to produce different notes.

Many brass instruments are "transposing" instruments. The score they play from must be revised or transposed according to which instrument they are playing. If the printed music isn't transposed, the player has to do the transposing as he or she is playing.

- **TRUMPET (AND CORNET AND BUGLE)**

The basic instrument in the brass family is the trumpet. It is the smallest member of the brass family and therefore plays the highest notes. Its clear, bright, penetrating sound is used for military marches and fanfares. It can be quieted with a plastic or cardboard mute placed into the bell (the opening furthest from the mouthpiece) which produces an expressively mournful, elegiac tone. Different kinds of mutes create different effects. The trumpet player blows into a mouthpiece shaped like a small cup, but it is the shape of the player's lips that creates the different pitches. The piping of the trumpet is curved and circles back on itself so that the player can easily hold it. The trumpet has three valves; the first valve lowers the pitch by a whole tone, the second valve changes the pitch by a half tone, and the third valve regulates it by a tone and a half.

Related to the trumpet are the bugle (used to give army signals) and the smaller cornet which has the same range as the trumpet and is

Appendix: Overview of the Orchestra

played in the same manner. The cornet has a richer, fuller tone than the trumpet and is featured in brass bands. A cornet player can play very fast music with ease. There is also a piccolo trumpet and a flugal horn. Each of these instruments is designed for a different kind of music and the trumpeter may have a small collection of instruments at his disposal.

- **FRENCH HORN**

The French horn is so-named because it was developed primarily in France from the hunting horn. It is a coiled and convoluted instrument with four full yards of tubing. The French horn has a large, bell-shaped opening at its mouth which the player thrusts his fist into, both to support the weight of the instrument and to help mute the notes. The French horn (or just "the horn" for short) has a full, warm, hunting-call sound with a three-octave range. The French horn has only three valves and a trigger, so the pitch is determined by the player's "embouchure" or mouth position, making this instrument particularly difficult to play.

Horn players are often seen in the orchestra turning their instruments upside down to drain them. What happens is this: when the player's warm breath meets the cold metal inside the horn, water vapor condenses, water drops accumulate, and these drops can dribble out of the instrument and onto the floor. Not lovely, but true. So horn players need strong stomachs.

- **TROMBONE (AND BASS TROMBONE, EUPHONIUM, AND BARITONE HORN)**

Unlike the other brass instruments, the trombone uses a siding section of tubing which the player moves in and out to produce the required notes. Because of its structure, the trombone produces a free and easy sound with a sliding, slippery quality. The trombone's tubing is about three yards long without the slide. With the slide extended, it grows to four yards. The player changes the length of the tubing and therefore the pitch of the note by moving the slide from first position to one of six other positions. Each of these positions is located at a fixed distance from the first position. The performer must find these positions by ear, without the help of markings on the slide itself. The sound of the trombone is one octave below the trumpet and is the tenor of the brass family.

Another member of the trombone family is the bass trombone which has larger pipes and sounds lower and heavier, but is played in an identical manner to the trombone. The bass trombone has a second attachment, another loop of piping, and another valve allowing the player to reach all the way down through the register of the tuba. Other members of this family are the euphonium (which actually looks more like a tuba) and the baritone horn. These two instruments have baritone voices with deep and mellow tones. The baritone horn is said to be the easiest instrument in the entire brass family to blow. The euphonium comes in two sizes, large and extra-large. (The extra-large size is called the double bass euphonium.)

- **TUBA (AND THE SOUSAPHONE)**

The tuba is the largest, fattest, and heaviest member of the brass family. It features some nine yards of tubing, twice the length of the tubing in a trombone. The mouthpiece of the tuba is very large and covers almost all of the player's lips. The tuba plays notes that are in a very low and limited range. Their sound might be described as large, smooth, fat or round. Some people compare a tuba's sound to that of an organ. The range of a tuba is an octave lower than the trombone. The tuba can be muted, although it requires a very large mute.

Related to the tuba is the sousaphone (which was designed so that it could be easily carried in a marching band) and the baritone, which is a smaller version of the tuba and is also used in brass bands. The sousaphone is the largest of all the brass instruments, named after John Philip Sousa, the 19th century American conductor who wrote marches such as *"The Stars and Stripes Forever."* The sousaphone is so big that it dwarfs its player.

Appendix: Overview of the Orchestra

THE PERCUSSION SECTION

The fourth and last of the orchestra sections is the percussion section, sometimes called the "kitchen department," since at one time pots and pans were used. The distinctive sounds of percussion instruments are made by hitting or stroking them. (The meaning of "percussion" is "hit" or "struck.") Because these instruments are struck, it is not difficult for a beginner to produce a satisfactory sound. It is, however, a challenge to play percussion instruments well and becoming proficient on them requires considerable musicianship. In addition, there is a large number of percussion instruments and the percussionist is required to master them all.

The best known of the percussion instruments is the drum which consists of a base made of wood or metal, over which a membrane of animal skin, cloth, or strong paper is stretched. The drum produces different notes, depending on how tightly the skin is stretched across its base. The tighter the skin is stretched, the higher the note sounds when the skin is hit.

The big drums are called "timpani" (the Italian word for "drums") and the performer is a "timpanist." He is the chief percussion performer and usually has four drums to tune and play at once. (The timpani are sometimes referred to as kettle drums because of their kitchen-kettle-like shape.) Each of the timpani can be tuned to a different note. Timpani have foot pedals that tighten and loosen the skin by means of metal rods. The timpanist needs an unusually good "ear" since he or she often has to tune four drums to different notes and do this while the orchestra is playing—no mean feat.

Other instruments in the drum family are the snare drum, the side drum, and the tom-tom. The snare drum comes in several sizes and is played with two sticks. Drum players usually do most of their practicing at home on a practice pad, a wooden block covered by a skin.

Technically, anything that can be hit could be a part of the percussion section. In addition to the drums, the usual percussion instruments are the triangle, chimes, cymbals, gong, wood blocks, clappers, maracas, castanets, tubular bells, and tambourine. These instruments are hit, banged, struck, crashed, scraped, clicked or shaken—whatever is called for. While the tympani are assigned to the tympanist, the other percussion players share the rest of the percussion instruments. Since they scurry from one instrument to another, these players must think, move, and act quickly.

Also included in the percussion section are the piano and its keyboard relatives—harpsichord, clavichord, xylophone, vibraphone, marimba, celeste, and the glockenspiel. The xylophone and marimba are made of a set of gradually longer rectangular wood blocks. The longer the block, the lower in pitch the note that sounds. The xylophone and marimba are played with two or more sticks or "mallets."

- **PIANO**

The piano, itself a percussion instrument, is in a class by itself. Its formal, proper name is the "piano-forte" which translates to English somewhat peculiarly as "soft-loud." Before the invention of the modern piano (by an Italian named Cristofori in the 18th century), the harpsichord could not produce soft and loud notes. All notes sounded at the same decibel level, which was soft by today's standards. Therefore, the invention of the piano-forte was a major breakthrough—the piano could play soft lullabies and loud marches equally well.

The piano is generally considered to be the basic instrument for the study of music, and it has a remarkably rich range of literature. The 88 keys of the piano are attached to 88 small hammers and wire strings. When the performer presses a key, the mechanism moves a hammer, which then strikes a set of strings, causing them to vibrate and create the sound. The piano is the basis for the study of theoretical music such as theory and composition and, as such, is a point of reference for all professional musicians.

Appendix: Overview of the Orchestra

- **HARP**

The angelic sounding harp is also classified as a percussion instrument since it is brushed or plucked with the fingers. Harpists sit on a chair or stool, leaning their instrument against their right shoulder. The harp has 47 strings of different lengths, each string producing a different note. The strings of the harp are attached to a board shaped like the sounding board inside of a piano and these strings are color-coded. Seven pedals are used to change the length (and therefore the pitch) of the strings. One pedal changes all of the C strings, another all of the D strings, and so forth. Each pedal has three positions: flat, natural, and sharp.

- **AN OVERVIEW**

One of the most helpful ways to get a real overview of the orchestral instruments is to listen to a recording of Benjamin Britten's *Young Person's Guide to the Orchestra*, which features a narrated tour of the orchestra, highlighting the unique sound of each instrument.

ENDNOTES

Chapter One

Chapter Two

[1] Holden, Anthony. *Tchaikovsky, A Biography.* New York: Random House, 1995.
[2] Wagner, Richard. *My Life.* New York: Da Capo Press, 1992.
[3] Marek, George. *Puccini, A Biography.* New York: Simon and Schuster, 1951.
[4] Scott, Michael. *The Great Caruso.* New York: Alfred A. Knopf, 1988.
[5] Fay, Laurel E. *Shostakovich, A Life.* New York: Oxford University Press, 2000.
[6] Plaskin, Glenn. *Horowitz: A Biography.* New York: William Morrow and Co., 1983.
[7] Robinson, Harlow. *Sergei Prokofiev, A Biography.* New York: Viking Press. 1987.
[8] Marek, George. *Schubert.* New York: Viking Penguin, Inc., 1985.
[9] Copland, Aaron, and Vivian Perlis. *Copland, 1900-1942.* New York: St. Martin's, 1984.
[10] Carreras, Jose. *Jose Carreras, Singing from the Soul, An Autobiography.* Los Angeles: Y.C.P. Publications, 1989.
[11] Goldberg, Isaac. *George Gershwin, A Study in American Music.* New York: Frederick Ungar Publishing Co., 1958.
[12] Kennedy, Michael. *Richard Strauss, Man, Musician, Enigma.* Cambridge: Cambridge University Press, 1999.
[13] Burton, Humphrey. *Yehudi Menuhim, A Life.* Boston: Northeastern University Press, 2000.
[14] Kirk, H.L. *Pablo Casals, A Biography.* New York: Holt, Rinehard and Winston, 1974.
[15] Walker, Alan. *Franz Liszt, The Virtuoso Years, 1811-1847.* New York: Alfred A. Knopf, 1983.
[16] Kennedy, Michael. *Mahler.* New York: Schirmer Books, 1990.
[17] Holden, Anthony. *Tchaikovsky, A Biography.* New York: Random House, 1995.
[18] Reich, Howard. *Van Cliburn.* Nashville: Thomas Nelson Publishers, 1993.
[19] Freidrich, Otto. *Glen Gould, A Life and Variations.* New York: Random House, 1989.
[20] Milhaud, Darius. *My Happy Life, An Autobiography.* London: Marion Boyars, 1995.
[21] Filar, Marian, and Charles Patterson. *From Buchenwald to Carnegie Hall.* Jackkson, Mississippi: University of Mississippi, 2002.
[22] Rogers, Richard. *Musical Stages, an Autobiography of Richard Rogers.* New York: Random House, 1975.
[23] Seroff, Victor. *Sergei Prokofiev, A Soviet Tragedy.* New York: Funk and Wagnalls, 1968.
[24] "This is Your Brain in Tune," *Yale University Magazine,* September/October, 2003.
[25] Slonimsky, Nicolas. *Perfect Pitch, A Life Story.* Oxford: Oxford University Press, 1988.
[26] Filar, Marian, and Charles Patterson. *From Buchenwald to Carnegie Hall.* Jackson, Mississippi: University of Mississippi, 2002.

[27] Griesinger, Georg August. *Joseph Haydn, 18th Century Gentleman and Genius.* Translated by Vernon Gotwals. Madison: University of Wisconsin Press, 1963.

Chapter Three
[28] Stern, Isaac, with Chaim Potok. *My First 79 Years.* New York: Alfred A. Knopf, 1999.
[29] Rampal, Jean-Pierre. *Music, My Love.* New York: Random House, 1989.
[30] Barenboim, Daniel, Michael Lewin, ed. *Baniel Barenboim, A Life in Music.* New York: Scribners and Sons, 1991.
[31] Collier, James Lincoln. *Benny Goodman and the Swing Era.* New York: Oxford University Press, 1989.
[32] Ma, Marina, as told to John A. Rallo. *My Son, Yo-Yo.* Hong Kong: Chinese University Press, 1995.
[33] Wilson, Elizabeth. *Jacqueline du Pré, Her Life, Her Music, Her Legend.* New Yori: Arcade Publishing, 1998.
[34] Filar, Marian, and Charles Patterson. *From Buchenwald to Carnegie Hall.* Jackson, Mississippi: University of Mississippi, 2002.

Chapter Four
[35] Ben-Tovim, Atarah and Douglas Boyd. *The Right Instrument for Your Child. A Practical Guide for Parents and Teachers.* New York: Quill William Morrow, 1985.

Chapter Five

Chapter Six
[36] "Bands Across America," Naperville, Illinois United School District.
[37] Catterall, James L., Richard Chapleau, and John Iwanaga. "Involvement in the Arts and Human Development: General Involvement and Intensive Involvement in Music and Theater Arts." Los Angeles, CA: The Imagination Project at UCLA Graduate School of Education and Information Studies, 1999.
[38] D.L. Hamann and L.M. Walker, "Music teachers as role models for African-American students," Journal of Research in Music Education, 41, 1993.

Chapter Seven
[39] Schonberg, Harold C. *Horowitz, His Life and Music.* New York: Simon and Schuster, 1992.
[40] James Burnett. *Ravel, His Life and Times.* New York: Midas Books, 1983.
[41] Horne, Marilyn, with Jane Scovell. *Marilyn Horne, My Life.* New York: Atheneum, 1983.
[42] Stern, Isaac, with Chaim Potok. *My First 79 Years.* New York: Alfred A. Knopf, 1999.
[43] Friedrich, Otto. *Glen Gould, A Life and Variations.* New York: Random House, 1989.
[44] Ruttencutter, Helen Drees. *Previn.* New York: St. Martin's/Marek, 1985.
[45] Milhaud, Darius. *My Happy Life, An Autobiography.* London: Marion Boyars, 1995.
[46] Whittall, Mary, ed. Andrew Gray, translator. *My Life, Richard Wagner.* New York: Da Capo Press, 1992.
[47] Larner, Gerald. *Maurice Ravel.* London, Phaidon Press, Ltd. 1996.
[48] Sutherland, Joan. *A Prima Donna's Progress, the Autobiography of Joan Sutherland.* Washington, D.C: Regnery Publishing, Inc., 1997.

[49] Fingleton, David. *Kiri Te Kanawa. A Biography.* New York: Atheneum, 1983.
[50] Horne, Marilyn, with Jane Scovell. *Marilyn Horne, My Life.* New York: Athemeum, 1983.
[51] Baldock, Robert. *Pablo Casals.* Boston: Northeastern University Press, 1992.

Chapter Eight
[52] Marek, Geroge. *Puccini, A Biography.* New York: Simon and Schuster, 1951.

Chapter Nine
[53] Phillips-Matz. *Verdi, A Biography.* New York: Oxford University Press, 1993.
[54] Volkov, Solomon, ed. *Testimony, the Memoires of Dmitri Shostakovich.* New York: Harper and Row, 1979.
[55] Curtiss, Mina. *Bizet and His World.* New York: Alfred A. Knopf, 1958.
[56] Daniel, Oliver. *Stokowski, A Counterpoint of View.* New York: Dodd, Mead and Co., 1982.

Chapter Ten
[57] Heyman, Barbara. *Samuel Barber, the Composer and His Music.* New York: Oxford University Press, 1992.
[58] Rorem, Ned. *Knowing When to Stop, A Memoir.* New York: Simon and Schuster, 1994.
[59] Solomon, Maynard. *Beethoven.* Second, Revised Edition. New York: Schirmer Books, 1998.
[60] Rampal, Jean-Pierre. *Music, My Love.* New York: William Morrow and Co., 1983.
[61] Landon, H.C. Robbins. *Handel And His World.* Boston: Little Brown, and Co., 1984.
[62] *Ibid.*
[63] *Ibid.*
[64] Clarson-Leach, Robert. *Berlioz, His Life and Times.* New York: Midas Books, 1983.
[65] Secrest, Meryle. *Leonard Bernstein, A Life.* New York: Alfred A. Knopf, 1994.
[66] *Ibid.*

Chapter Eleven
[67] Thomas, Lewis, "The Case for Music in the Schools," *Phi Delta Kappa,* February, 1994.
[68] Graziano, Amy, Matthew Peterson, and Gordon Shaw, "Enhanced learning of proportional math through music training and spatial-temporal training." *Neurological Research 21,* March, 1999.
[69] *NELS:88, National Education Longitudinal Survey.*
[70] Catterall, James S., Richard Chapleau, and John Iwanaga. *"Involvement in the Arts and Human Development: General Involvement and Intensive Involvement and Music and Theater Arts."* Los Angeles, CA: The Imagination Project at UCLA Graduate School of Education and Information Studies, 1999.
[71] Rauscher, Frances H., Gordon Shaw, Katherine N. Ky, "Listening to Mozart enhances spatial-temporal reasoning: towards a neurophysiological basis," University of California, Irvine, 1994.
[72] Rauscher, Shaw, Levine, Ky and Wright, *"Music and Spatial Task Performance: A Causal Relationship,"* University of California, Irvine, 1994.
[73] Gromko, J.E., and Poorman, A.S. (1998) "The effect of music training on preschoolers' spatial-temporal tast performance." Journal of Research in Music Education, 46, 173-181.

[74] Rauscher, F.H., Shaw, G.L., Levine, L.J., Wright, E.L., Dennis, W.R., and Newcomb, R. "Music training causes long-term enhancement of preschool children's spatial-temporal reasoning." Neurological Research, 19, 1-8, 1997.

[75] Rauscher, F.H., and Zupan, M.A. (1999). Classroom keyboard instruction improves kindergarten children's spatial-temporal performance: A field study. Manuscript in press, Early Childhood Research Quarterly.

[76] Dr. Agnes S. Chan of the Chinese University of Hong Kong, published in July, 2003 in the journal *Neuropsychology.*

[77] Carl Hartman, "Arts May Improve Students' Grades," *The Associated Press*, October, 1999.

[78] *Ibid.*

[79] Texas Music Educators Association, 1988-1996.

[80] *College-Bound Seniors National Report: Profile of SAT Program Test Takers.* Princeton, NJ: The College Entrance Examination Board, 2001.

[81] The National Education Longitudinal Study of 1988, First Follow-up, 1990, Second Follow-Up, 1992, National Center for Education Statistics, Washington, DC.

[82] Gardiner, Martin F.,Alan Fox, Donna Jeffrey and Faith Knowles, as reported in *Nature*, May 23, 1996.

[83] Patterson, A. 2993. Music Educators Journal, 89(4), 35-38.

[84] According to Dr. Mark Tramo, Assistant Professor of Neurology, Harvard Medical School.

[85] Susan Block, "The Musical Mind," *The American School Board Journal*, January, 1997.

[86] Edmund Rothstein, "Music on Their Minds," *New York Times*, November 17, 1996.

[87] Frank Wilson, *The Hand: How It Shapes the Brain, Language, and Culture.*

[88] Schlaug, G., Jancke, L., Huang, Y., and Steinmetz, H., 1994. In vivo morphometry of interhem ispheric asymmetry and connectivity in musicians. In I. Deliege (Ed.), Proceedings of the 3rd international conference for musicperception and cognition (pp. 417-418). Liege, Belgium.

[89] Grant Venerable, *"The Paradox of the Silicon Savior,"* as reported in *"The Case for Sequential Music Education in the Core Curriculum of the Public Schools,"* The Center for the Arts in the Basic Curriculum, New York, 1989.

[90] Weinberger, Norm. "Cortical Activation Patterns during Complex Motor Tasks in Piano Players and Control Subjects. A Functional Magnetic Resonance Imaging Study." *Neuroscience Letters* 278, no. 3(2000): 189-93.

[91] Ratey John J., MD. *A User's Guide to the Brain.* New York: Pantheon Books, 2001.

[92] Milgram, R.M., Hong, E. In*: Subotnik, R., Arnold K., eds. Longitudinal Studies in Contemporary Gifted Education.* Norwood, N.J.

[93] Gregory Annig.

Chapter Twelve

[94] Texas Commission on Drug and Alcohol Abuse Report. Reported in the Houston Chronicle, January, 1998.

[95] National Education Longitudinal Study, Second Follow-Up, 1992.

[96] *Collier, p.13.*

[97] "Music Linked to Reduced Criminality," *MuSICA* Research Notes, Winter, 2000.

[98] According to Mark Mazzaferro, Public Information Officer for the city, winter of 2001.

[99] MENC—The National Association for Music Education, Reston, Virginia "Music Education Facts and Figures, 2002."

[100] "Rhythm as Key to Music's Evolutionary Role in Human Intellectual Development," Center for Timing Coordination, and Motor Skills, 2000.
[101] "Cassily Column," TCAMS Professional Resource Center, 2000.
[102] 1990 Report of the National Commission on Music Education.
[103] General Norman Schwartzkopf, United States Army, as reported by the Naperville, Illinois, Community Unit School District 203, "Resources and Information for Music Advocacy."
[104] Baylor College of Medicine, Houston, Texas.
[105] As reported in the *British Medical Journal*, 1996.
[106] National Arts Education Research Center, New York University, 1990.
[107] N.H. Barry, Project ARISE: Meeting the needs of disadvantaged students through the arts, Auburn University, 1992.
[108] In an address to the National Assembly of MENC, The National Association for Music Educators, July, 1999.

INDEX

A

All-State Band 96
Alp horn 78
Amadeus 13
American Youth Symphony 104
Anti-social behavior 192
Anxiety 56, 197, 200
Arrowbear Music Camp 5, 115
Attention 21, 37, 51, 64, 95, 98, 121, 155, 170, 180, 181, 203, 204
Auditioning 157, 158, 164, 197, 199
Authority 134, 143, 178

B

Bamboo 62
Bands 64, 84, 85, 92, 94, 191
Barber, Samuel 167, 223
Barenboim, Daniel 37
Baritone 168, 170, 174, 215
Bar Mitzvah 19, 146
Basketball 86, 88, 89, 90, 194, 201
Bass 8, 32, 39, 40, 41, 42, 43, 45, 53, 55, 56, 57, 71, 73, 78, 79, 97, 149, 158, 164, 179, 180, 190, 209, 215
Bassists 47, 97
Bassoon 33, 47, 58, 63, 113, 115, 149, 190, 209, 210, 211, 213
Beethoven, Ludwig 23, 161, 168, 171, 192, 223
Belonging 190
Berlioz, Hector 170
Bernstein, Leonard 170, 171, 223
Bizet 151, 223
Boredom 195

Bow 33, 34, 73, 104, 129
Braces 35, 66
Brass instruments 64, 65, 69, 108
Burnout 133
Busking 147

C

Campbell, Don 185
Cane 62
Carnegie Hall 103, 171, 221, 222
Carnyx 78
Carreras, Jose 17, 221
Caruso 14, 18, 221
Casals, Pablo 19, 124, 221, 223
Cases 3, 16, 55, 56, 78, 120, 122, 166
Cello 35, 36, 38, 40, 42, 43, 44, 46, 47, 53, 55, 56, 79, 120, 134, 137, 139, 149, 162, 208, 209
Center for Timing, Coordination, and Motor Skills 194
Cerebellum 187
Chairs 95, 97, 98
Chamber music 6, 31, 72, 83, 110, 111, 115, 138, 156, 164
Chang, Sarah 16
Channon 44
Character-building 193
Clarinet 3, 33, 35, 41, 48, 58, 59, 60, 62, 78, 90, 92, 94, 118, 140, 146, 160, 178, 210, 212, 213
Cleveland Institute of Music 148
Colburn School of Music 137, 148
College 7, 10, 11, 47, 56, 62, 86, 94, 96, 120, 129, 130, 142, 153, 164, 165, 168, 170, 173, 183, 186, 201, 233

227

Color 26, 46
Commitment 48, 114, 134, 149, 174, 179, 180, 188, 195
Communication 179, 195
Competitions 31, 128, 133, 148, 158, 161, 163, 164, 174, 198
Composition 118, 188
Concentration 64, 103, 136, 179
Concert 1, 6, 17, 18, 34, 37, 41, 67, 86, 88, 90, 96, 100, 116, 143, 155, 202
Concertmaster 172
Conflicts 87, 88
Conflicts of interest 166
Cooperation 192, 198
Coordination 194, 225
Copland, Aaron 17
Cornet 78, 214
Craft 142, 180
Curtis Institute of Music 133

D

Decision-making 163, 194
Defeat 161
Directions 32, 72, 177, 178, 179
Disappointment 173, 198
Discipline 53, 102, 106, 177, 178, 179, 180, 188, 193, 196
Dorothy Chandler Pavilion 1
Double bass 73
Drugs 152, 191, 201
Drum 78, 160, 217
Du Pre, Jacqueline 222
Dynamics ii, 194

E

eBay 74
Einstein, Albert 181
Elvis 19, 21
Embouchure 42, 92
Emotions 37, 159, 204
English horn 61, 211, 212, 213
Ensemble 159, 160
Epstein, David 186

Euphonium 47, 48, 49, 215
Excellence 66, 95, 112, 124, 125, 129, 140, 175, 177, 180, 197

F

Failure 161, 169, 197
Fears 197
Feedback 164, 180, 202
Feynman, Richard 181
Filar, Marian 23, 27, 44
Fingers 23, 24, 30, 31, 56, 59, 63, 64, 104, 133, 170, 185
Flute 3, 4, 5, 6, 7, 8, 11, 33, 34, 35, 37, 39, 42, 45, 46, 58, 59, 60, 74, 77, 80, 83, 90, 97, 100, 101, 110, 116, 118, 135, 138, 156, 159, 160, 165, 167, 169, 170, 196, 210, 211, 213
French horn 33, 41, 42, 43, 45, 47, 67, 68, 69, 78, 115, 161, 172, 190, 193, 213, 214, 215
Frustration 54, 111, 167, 195

G

"Good ear" 53, 59, 64, 66, 67, 70
Gershwin, George 18, 221
Goals 116, 175, 180
Goodman, Benny 40, 191, 222
Gould, Glenn 22, 24
Gratification 54, 175, 193, 195
Guarneri del Gesu 149
Guitar 21, 34, 36, 78

H

Handel, George Frederick 169
Harp 70, 79, 219
Harvard University 183, 185
Haydn, Joseph 34, 222
Heifetz, Jascha 16
High school 7, 8, 9, 10, 11, 33, 48, 49, 60, 70, 71, 84, 86, 87, 88, 89, 90, 92, 95, 96, 97, 98, 102, 106, 116, 119, 120, 121, 122, 129, 135, 141, 145, 158, 163,

167, 170, 174, 181, 184, 190, 191, 233
Hobby 86, 201
Homework 5, 8, 9, 10, 87, 106, 113
Horn 17, 18, 33, 41, 42, 43, 45, 47, 61, 64, 67, 68, 69, 78, 91, 115, 121, 122, 150, 160, 161, 167, 172, 190, 193
Horne, Marilyn 103, 124, 222, 223
Horowitz, Vladimir 15, 102

I

Improvising 194
Incentives 108, 116
Insurance 79, 147, 148, 149
Internet 74, 75
Intonation 53, 66

J

Jazz 48, 56, 66, 89, 113
Joplin, Scott 25
Juilliard 57

K

Kennedy Center 148
Kettle drums 70
Keys 22, 23, 27, 30, 31, 63, 65, 117

L

Lanza, Mario 18
Left-handedness 53
Levers 58
Liszt, Franz 15, 19, 221
Loss 5, 39, 57, 79, 90, 141, 199
Los Angeles Philharmonic ii, 2, 8, 17, 130

M

Ma, Marina 41
Ma, Yo-Yo 38
Mahler, Gustav 20
Maintenance 4, 67, 80, 148
Mallets 39, 70

Marek, George 16
Marimba 69
Mathematics 16, 87, 182, 187
Maturity 16, 52, 131, 197, 199
Mentor x, 130
Menuhin, Yehudi 15, 18, 100
Metropolitan Youth Symphony Orchestra 157
Middle school 40, 47, 73, 86, 92, 93, 101, 119, 120, 121, 141, 181
Milhaud, Darius 23, 109
Mommy and Me classes 2, 34
Money 5, 49, 61, 74, 78, 93, 97, 98, 100, 117, 118, 119, 130, 131, 134, 135, 141, 146, 147, 148, 150, 151, 157, 171, 172, 173, 175, 203
Mouthpiece 36, 39, 41, 48, 60, 64, 68
Mozart 13, 23, 45, 86, 172, 182, 185, 186, 202, 223
Mr. Holland's Opus 91
Musicianship 96, 150, 165, 180
Music of the Heart 91
Music Teachers National Association 127, 128
Mute 67

N

National Cello Institute 107
National Commission on Music Education 196, 225
New England Conservatory of Music 171

O

Oberlin School of Music 171
Oboe 3, 30, 39, 42, 47, 48, 58, 60, 61, 62, 63, 91, 96, 118, 121, 141, 160, 210, 211, 212, 213
Orchestration 188
Outlet 201

P

Paganini Violin Competition 148

229

Pasadena Youth Symphony Orchestra 6
Pedals 14, 72
Perfect pitch 25, 221
Performance anxiety 197
Perlman, Itzhak 15, 38
Perseverance 188, 198
Phoenix Symphony 135
Piano 2, 4, 14, 15, 18, 19, 20, 21, 22, 23, 25, 26, 27, 28, 29, 30, 31, 32, 33, 34, 37, 38, 44, 46, 48, 53, 68, 71, 72, 78, 91, 94, 107, 108, 110, 111, 114, 116, 117, 118, 121, 122, 131, 138, 149, 151, 153, 154, 170, 171, 181, 183, 201, 218, 219
Piccolo 69, 78, 211
Pipes 169
Pitch 25, 221
Pittsburgh Symphony 46
Planck, Max 181
Plan B 11
Plato 205
Practice log 109, 116
Practicing 5, 8, 9, 10, 11, 62, 70, 71, 84, 90, 99, 100, 101, 102, 103, 104, 105, 106, 107, 108, 109, 110, 111, 112, 113, 114, 115, 116, 117, 119, 120, 121, 122, 123, 124, 135, 138, 151, 165, 174, 187, 191
Precocity 15
Previn, Andre 108
Pride 11, 63, 151, 188, 202
Principal 8, 9, 10, 11, 47, 94, 97, 129, 135, 137, 167, 172
Problem-solving 182, 194
Prodigy 15, 103
Prokofiev, Sergei 15, 24, 221
Puccini 14, 131, 132, 221, 223

Q

Quitting 99, 100, 101, 119, 122, 124

R

Rampal, Jean-Pierre 37, 169
Ravel, Maurice 117, 222
Reasoning 16, 177, 182, 183, 185, 223, 224
Reeds 60, 61, 62, 63, 64
Register 59, 66
Relative pitch 26
Repertoire 31, 32, 65, 205
Rewards 116
Rhythm 17, 34, 70, 185, 187, 188, 205
Riley, Richard W. 205
Risk 57, 58, 71, 79, 88, 203, 204
Rogers, Richard 23, 221
Rorem, Ned 168

S

Sacrifice 146, 151, 193
Salary 172, 173
SATs 165, 184, 188, 224
Saxophone 49, 50, 118
Scales 45, 91, 97, 102, 109, 110, 114, 196
Scholarships 147, 148, 164, 197
Schopenhauer 16
Schumann, Robert 20
Self-awareness 203
Self-confidence 126, 198
Self-discipline 106, 179, 196
Self-esteem 190, 195, 199, 202, 203
Self-expression 200
Self-motivation 107, 188
Self-reflection 203
Sensitivity 16, 18, 28, 66, 192
Shoplifting 191
Shostakovich 14, 151, 221
Shyness 197
Singing 18, 21, 221
Slides 36, 66, 67
Slonimsky, Nicolas 26
Soccer 36, 83, 89, 107, 120, 137, 155, 192
Soul 200, 205
Southern Californian Honor Orchestra 46

Sports 8, 32, 36, 87, 88, 89, 98, 120, 195, 201
Stage fright 199
Stage mothers 151
Stern, Isaac 37, 103
Stick-to-it-iveness 195
Stokowski, Leopold 157
Stradivari Society 149
Strauss, Richard 18, 221
String bass 8, 40, 43, 45, 56, 149
String instrument 32, 44, 53, 55, 57, 66, 75, 207
Studio 128, 129, 130, 172
Sutherland, Joan 122, 222
Suzuki 46, 53, 114, 136
Swimming 90

T

Tchaikovsky 13, 14, 21, 23, 26, 221
Teamwork 90
Tenor 14, 66, 79
Te Kanawa, Kiri 124, 223
Theory 121
Thespians 84, 192
Timbre 46
Timing 194, 225
Toastmasters 199
Tone 25, 27, 44, 45, 53, 58, 68, 132, 169, 188, 194, 196
Transposing 25
Triangle 70
Trombone 36, 40, 41, 42, 43, 48, 65, 66, 67, 79, 108, 115, 118, 158, 214, 215, 216
Trumpet 3, 35, 41, 42, 45, 65, 66, 69, 74, 78, 84, 89, 91, 92, 93, 95, 108, 116, 137, 156, 159, 162, 213, 214, 215, 216
Tuba 36, 41, 42, 43, 47, 48, 49, 50, 64, 69, 74, 78, 93, 94, 173, 214, 216
Turner, Ted 193
Tutors 181
Tympani 69

U

United States Department of Education 181
University of Hong-Kong 183, 224

V

Validation 203
Values 32, 46, 109, 193
Valves 66, 68
Van Cliburn 22
Verdi, Guiseppe 150
Verdi's Requiem 1
Viola 38, 39, 41, 42, 43, 44, 53, 55, 75, 76, 77, 85, 200, 209
Violin 3, 18, 21, 32, 33, 34, 35, 36, 37, 38, 39, 41, 42, 43, 44, 47, 48, 53, 54, 55, 56, 58, 71, 75, 76, 89, 90, 91, 100, 104, 106, 109, 116, 120, 121, 123, 134, 135, 148, 160, 166, 168, 174, 179, 181, 201, 203, 204, 208
Virtuoso 86, 221
Voice 32, 39, 45, 46, 59, 63, 72, 141, 174, 200

W

Wagner 14, 26, 110, 221, 222
Waitlist 129
Woodwind instruments 58, 210
Work ethic 64, 193, 194, 195
Wunderkind 14, 15, 22

X

Xylophone 69

Y

Young Musicians Foundation 126, 148, 164
Youth orchestras 94, 95, 96, 97, 111, 138, 153, 192

About The Author

Michelle Siteman has a BA from the University of Chicago and a master's degree from Yale University. She has thirty years of experience teaching at the grade school, high school and college levels, and she currently coaches and trains new teachers at colleges in southern California. A music lover and the mother of three grown children, Ms. Siteman writes of the rewards and challenges of raising a musical child with the clarity and insight of a teacher and with the heart of a mother. Jonathan, the youngest of her children, is well on his way to a career in classical music.

She can be contacted at her website: www.michellesiteman.com